D1319720

# PHILADELPHIA

## A CHRONOLOGICAL & DOCUMENTARY HISTORY

# 1615 - 1970

Compiled and Edited by
## ADRIENNE SIEGEL

Series Editor
HOWARD B. FURER

1975
OCEANA PUBLICATIONS, INC.
Dobbs Ferry, New York

Library of Congress Cataloging in Publication Data

Siegel, Adrienne.
  Philadelphia.

  (American cities chronology series)
  Bibliography: p.
  Includes index.
  SUMMARY: A chronology of important events and people
in Philadelphia accompanied by pertinent documents.
    1. Philadelphia--History--Chronology. ~~2. Philadel-
phia--History--Sources.~~ I. Title
  F158.3.S53         974.8'11          74-23205
  ISBN 0-379-00621-9

974.811
Si15

## TABLE OF CONTENTS

For my Father

# EDITOR'S FOREWORD

This text has been compiled as a research tool for the student interested in readily discovering some of the key developments that have shaped the history of Philadelphia. By surveying many of the pivotal events that have contributed to Philadelphia's complex formation and by presenting pertinent documents as well as a critical bibliography, the editor has attempted to throw a light on some of the broad themes and patterns of a highly creative urban community. It is hoped that this introductory guide will be used by the student as a springboard for further explorations into the "personality" of one of America's most important cities. The most accurate dates possible have been cited. However, the student is urged to go back to the original sources in case of a conflict.

Adrienne Siegel
Little Swartswood Lake
Sussex County, New Jersey

## PHILADELPHIA IN THE COLONIAL PERIOD
### 1615-1776

1615      Cornelius Hendricksen, navigator from the Netherlands, views the site of Philadelphia early in the year.

1623      Hendricksen establishes a Dutch trading post and stockade on the site of the future city.

1638      William Usselinex brings the first Swedish immigrants to settle along the Delaware River.

1654      The Swedes surrender to a Dutch force sent from New York and pledge their allegiance to the Netherlands. The families of this group become part of the original settlers of William Penn's Philadelphia.

1677      Early in the year Swede's Church, the first church in Philadelphia, is erected.

1678      English and Scottish Quakers, arriving on the ship Shield, settle near the site of Philadelphia.

1681      March 24. William Penn receives title to Pennsylvania in a land grant from King Charles II. He pledges to provide an asylum for the persecuted members of the Society of Friends, as well as for the oppressed of all nations who want to live in accordance with the principles of peace and purity.

         October. Penn appoints a commission of William Crispin, Nathaniel Allen and John Bezar to cooperate with Governor Markham in laying out the site for a "great city." They are instructed by Penn to select a location with suitable water frontage on the Delaware River, so that the new town can serve as a seaport. The streets are to be laid out in a straight and regular pattern with spaces reserved for markets and squares.

1682      Philadelphia is chosen as the name of the new city to be created. Its name, meaning "City of Brotherly Love," is copied from a city of Asia Minor mentioned in St. John's Apocalypse.

         John Key, the first child of English parentage to be born in Philadelphia, is delivered during the winter. Penn, in recognition of this event, presents him with a plot of land in the city.

March 10. Land titles are given for the first time to Germans whom Penn wants to recruit to his colony. As an additional inducement, city lots are offered to these first German purchasers.

April. Thomas Holme lays out the city of Philadelphia with geometrical precision. Vine Street becomes the northern boundary and Cedar Street the southern. The main thoroughfare, extending from east to west, is named Market Street and a street of the same width, running north to south, is call Broad Street. At the intersection of these two major avenues, a ten acre square is earmarked as the site for various public buildings and a Friends' Meeting House.

September 1. William Penn sets sail in the Welcome with a large congregation of Quakers for the colony of Pennsylvania.

October 27. William Penn arrives at New Castle.

December. Penn's "Great Law" is established for the province by the first legislature, which meets at Chester. The rights to vote is extended to all Christians, and freedom of worship is granted to all inhabitants. The "Frame of Government" keeps political control in the hands of the proprictor and the Free Society of Traders. The elected general assembly is empowered to approve or reject bills proposed by the governor and provincial council.

1683　　　Holmes' Portraiture of the City of Philadelphia in the Province of Pennsilvania in America is published and sold in England.

Penn establishes a court to naturalize foreigners.

March 10. The governor and council establish Philadelphia as the seat of government and capital of Pennsylvania.

June. Francis Daniel Pastorius, a scholar, historian and poet, sails for Philadelphia and becomes the first German settler in Germantown. His emigration is followed by many others from Krefeld.

June. Shackamaxon Treaty establishes peaceful relations between the Quakers and Indian tribes

August. Approximately eighty families are housed within the city.

October 12. Pastorius is granted a warrant for 6,000 acres of land.

October 25. Pastorius divides his land among many German settlers.

December 26. The provincial council encourages education for the youth of Philadelphia by authorizing Enoch Flower to open a school.

1684      Penn writes a prayer for the city, asking that this virgin settlement be protected from evil and remain steadfast in righteousness.

1685      The population grows to approximately 2,500 .

Caves in Philadelphia, originally used as temporary shelters, become disorderly taverns and are shut down by municipal authorities.

The council authorizes the development of ferry transportation across the Schuylkill River at Market Street.

October. William Bradford sets up the first printing press in the colonies. He issues a pamphlet entitled "The Kalendarium Pennsilvaniense, or America's Messenger, Being an Almanack for the year 1686. Published by Samuel Atkins."

1687      William Rittenhuysen, a Mennonite preacher, arrives with his family. His son David, who changes his surname to Rittenhouse, later becomes a prominent astronomer.

The council marks the harbor and channel by buoys; it lays out roads between the city and surrounding countryside; it establishes the first permanent jail on Second Street, near Market Street.

February. William Penn withdraws executive power from the council and places it in a commission composed of Nicholas More, Thomas Lloyd, James Claypoole, John Eckley, and Robert Turner. However, dissension continues to wrack the colony.

1689        The first public school is established in Philadelphia. It
            develops into the William Penn Charter School.

1690        A paper-mill is established by William Rittenhuysen on
            Wissahickon Creek.

            January. Blackwell is recalled as governor, and Thomas
            Lloyd is selected by the council as its president.

1691        Penn commissions Thomas Lloyd to serve as deputy govern-
            or of Pennsylvania.

            Penn signs a charter for Philadelphia and appoints Humphrey
            Morrey as mayor. However, the proprietor remains in
            England and ignores this instrument of government, address-
            ing the governor and council in regard to municipal affairs.

1692        William and Mary issue a patent to Benjamin Fletcher to
            take control of Pennsylvania, when they become suspicious
            that William Penn is intriguing for the restoration of James
            II. The Quakers of Pennsylvania refuse to cooperate with
            Fletcher when asked to supply funds and troops for war
            against France and the Indians on the frontier.

1693        A town-market, to operate on Wednesdays and Saturdays,
            is constructed at the intersection of Market and Second
            streets.

1694        William and Mary reinstate William Penn as proprietor of
            Pennsylvania.

1696        The Episcopalian Christ Church is completed.

1698        Christ Church begins a book collection that is to be used
            for a private library.

1699        Summer. Many die from the "Barbadoes distemper," a
            form of yellow fever.

            December 3. William Penn returns to his colony and re-
            sumes his role as governor.

1700        The Assembly passes a quarantine law, requiring ships with
            epidemic victims to remain a mile outside of Philadelphia
            until the vessel became free of contagion.

Old Swedes' Church is dedicated as Gloria Dei.

January. Penn rents the Slate Roof House, the largest private residence in the city, from Samuel Carpenter.

1701        Autumn. Penn appoints Andrew Hamilton to serve as lieutenant-governor. He selects James Logan to act as provincial secretary and clerk of the council, as well as to manage all of his interests in the colony.

October 25. Penn grants the city a charter of incorporation. Edward Shippen is chosen as Philadelphia's first true mayor. The charter sets up a corporation, which is to meet annually. The mayor, recorder, and aldermen are authorized to pass laws, ordinances, and constitutions for the governance of the city.

October 28. William Penn presents the Constitution of 1701 at Philadelphia prior to his departure to England. The most important governing charter for Pennsylvania until 1776, it changes the formerly elected council to a body appointed by the proprietor. Voting is restricted to property owners, freedom or worship guaranteed, but office holding limited to professed Christians.

1704        February. John Evans assumes the office of governor in Philadelphia. He is extremely unpopular.

1706        March. The first Presbytery is formed by seven ministers.

1707        The Philadelphia Association is established by Baptists.

February. David Lloyd, acting as the self-appointed defender of the people's liberties against the supposed greed of the proprietor, influences the members of the assembly to vote against the governor's request for any appropriations for defense and to petition Penn in strong language to remove Evans.

February. The assembly initiates impeachment proceedings against James Logan, the spokesman of both Penn and his appointee, Governor Evans, but the governor refuses to try the case.

1708        Colonel Charles Gookin is appointed lieutenant governor.

1710          David Lloyd and his followers are ousted from office in an election that reflects popular indignation at his scheme to seize the land of German settlers on a legal technicality. Lloyd leaves Philadelphia and settles in Chester.

              A Court House and Town Hall are erected on Market Street, between Second and Third streets.

              Pigs are banished from the city streets.

1712          Goats are prohibited from roaming the streets.

              The first American-built ocean liner is constructed in Philadelphia.

1716          The first iron forge in Pennsylvania is built by Thomas Rutter on Manatawny Creek.

1717          Armstrong Smith is granted a ferry monopoly on two points of the Delaware.

              May 31. William Keith assumes the commission of lieutenant governor from Hannah Penn, the widow of the proprietor. He is an able executive and maintains cordial relations with the assembly.

1718          June 24. The assembly passes a bill requiring those who receive public charity to wear a badge on their clothing with the letter "P" for pauper.

1719          Bricks are used for paving the sidewalks.

              December 22. The American Weekly Mercury, established by Andrew Bradford, becomes Philadelphia's first newspaper.

1722          October. Benjamin Franklin establishes residence in Philadelphia.

1724          The Carpenters' Company of Philadelphia establishes an association for craftsmen along the lines of a European guild.

1725          David Evans establishes the first regular transporation line for passengers running from Chestnut Street to Germantown, Frankford, and Gray's Ferry.

1726   Jews are given the right to own land and participate in business on a basis of equality with Christians.

      June 22. Major Patrick Gordon replaces William Keith as governor, following the latter's unpopular alignment with David Lloyd. The new governor reinstates James Logan as secretary of the provincial council.

1728   Benjamin Franklin founds The Junto, a secret society which debates contemporary political, literary, social, and scientific issues.

      May 28. Governor Gordon renews treaties of amity with the Indian tribes.

1729   September 25. Benjamin Franklin starts his own newspaper, The Pennsylvania Gazette. A one man enterprise, he sets the type, writes the stories, and delivers the paper to his subscribers.

1730   A site for a State House is selected on Chestnut Street, between Fifth and Sixth streets.

      The largest fire in Philadelphia's first half-century of development destroys $30,000 worth of property.

1731   Bartram's Garden is built near Gray's Ferry.

      The Library Company of Philadelphia is started by Benjamin Franklin. Financed by subscription fees, it is the first public library in North America.

      Dr. Thomas Cadwalader presents anatomical demonstrations to medical students.

1732   St. Joseph's Church, the first Catholic house of worship in the city, is established in Willing's Alley.

      A stage line to New York is begun.

      A social club for fishermen, the State in Schuylkill, is founded.

      A social club for people of Welsh origin, Fort St. David's,

is founded and governed by military rules.

Philadelphia opens its first public asylum for the poor, the first such almshouse in the Colonies.

Construction begins on the new State House.

1733     Hannah Penn, the executive of the Penn estate, dies and is succeeded in the proprietorship by her sons.

1736     The assembly opens its session in the newly constructed State House.

Benjamin Franklin receives his first public office, clerk of the assembly.

James Logan becomes governor upon the death of Patrick Gordon and serves for two years.

Franklin organizes a volunteer fire department, the Union Fire Company.

September and October. A treaty of peace and amity with the Indian tribes is concluded in a Great Council at the Friends' Meeting House. Negotiated under the influence of James Logan, it creates good will at a time when the other colonies are endangered by imminent Indian uprisings.

1737     Benjamin Franklin is appointed deputy postmaster general at Philadelphia, a lucrative post which brings profitable orders to his printing business.

1738     The first Jewish cemetery is established on Spruce Street, east of Ninth Street.

June 1. Colonel George Thomas, a West Indian planter, becomes governor and serves until 1746.

1739     November. The first privateer, the George, sets sail from Philadelphia under the initiative of Governor Thomas. It captures a full cargo, primarily of cocoa, from Spanish merchantmen.

The manufacture of wallpaper is introduced to the colonies by Plunkett Fleeson of Philadelphia.

1740   From 1740 to 1747 the Pennsylvania Assembly, under the influence of Quakers, refuses to vote defense appropriations while the Colonies are at war with Spain and France.

     The College of Philadelphia, initiated by Benjamin Franklin as a small charity school, becomes the fifth oldest college in the United States.

     April 14. War with Spain is announced in the city and volunteers for raids against the Spanish West Indies requested. However, the Quakers resist, and the assembly refuses appropriations for the support of the levies.

     November. George Whitefield gathers a large and enthusiastic following. He preaches in the New Building, a chapel especially erected by the populace who want to hear his unconventional sermons.

1741   Philadelphia struggles with the problems of a yellow fever epidemic, currency chaos, and business instability.

     January. Andrew Bradford publishes the first magazine in the colonies, the American Magazine.

     January. Franklin begins publication of a literary journal three days later, the General Magazine, but it survives for only six months.

1742   William Bradford launches the city's third newspaper, the Pennsylvania Journal and Weekly Advertiser.

     A puppet show is held in the city.

     The Library Company of Philadelphia is chartered and housed in the residence of Robert Grace in Pewter Platter Alley. Serving as "the mother of all the North American subscription libraries," its collection is enhanced by the gifts and selections of James Logan.

1743   Christopher Sauer publishes the first Bible in a foreign language in the Colonies. Printed in German, the 1,200 copies sell with difficulty.

1744   Franklin reprints Samuel Richardson's Pamela, the first novel to be published in America.

Franklin's Junto is transformed into the American Philosophical Society.

Every house in the city is provisioned with its own well, and water pumps are installed at every fifty paces of the streets.

1745    October. James Hamilton, the son of Andrew Hamilton, the famous Philadelphia lawyer who defended Peter Zenger, is chosen mayor and serves until October 1746.

William Logan, Chief Justice of Pennsylvania, originates the Loganian Library of Philadelphia.

1746    Christopher Sauer publishes a German periodical, the first foreign language newspaper in the Thirteen Colonies.

1747    The first Jewish congregation, Mikve Israel, is organized.

Benjamin Franklin attempts to arouse public sentiment against the defenselessness of Philadelphia by publishing a pamphlet, the "Plain Truth; or Serious Considerations of the Present State of the City of Philadelphia and Province of Pennsylvania by a Tradesman of Philadelphia."

November 21. A conference is held in response to Franklin's pamphlet, and it drafts a petition to the proprietary government, requesting that it send military equipment to the colony. Despite Quaker disapproval, preparations for defense are begun, and Franklin's Association destroys the non-resistance policy of the Quakers.

1748    James Hamilton is commissioned as lieutenant governor by the sons of William Penn. Although he is popular, he encounters conflict with the assembly when the legislative body attempts to expand the paper currency.

A dance is held by one of the early social clubs, The Philadelphia Assembly.

October 4. Benjamin Franklin is elected to the common council and pleas for reform of the night watch.

1749    St. Andrew's Society is founded to extend assistance to Scottish immigrants in Philadelphia.

Benjamin Franklin's pamphlet, Proposals Relating to the Education of Youth in Pennsylvania, stimulates the establishment of the Pennsylvania Academy, a school which later forms the nucleus of the University of Pennsylvania.

Philadelphia enjoys its first dramatic performance when the Murray-Kean theatrical company of England stages a production in the city.

1750    Benjamin Franklin is elected as representative of Philadelphia County to the assembly. He serves ten years consecutively.

Pennsylvania Hospital, the first such institution for the care of the sick in the United States, is originated by Benjamin Franklin. A site is selected on Eight Street, between Pine and Spruce streets.

Benjamin Franklin proposes a plan to improve the water supply. In place of noisome town pumps, he suggests a system of distribution from a central plant. Water pumped to an elevation, then could flow by gravity to wherever pipes would be laid.

1751    A line of packet boats makes regular runs to New York City.

The Pennsylvania Hospital is granted a charter.

A night watch is ordered. Plans are made for illuminating the streets.

October 1. Benjamin Franklin is elected alderman.

1752    April 13. The Philadelphia Contributionship for the Insurance of Houses from Loss by Fire is organized. The company's medal is placed on the doors of the insured homes. It is the first fire insurance company in America.

1753    Benjamin Franklin is appointed by the Pennsylvania legislature to persuade the crown to free the colony of proprietary rule.

1754    The London Coffee House is built on Front and Market streets. It becomes a meeting ground of local merchants to discuss the latest business news and negotiate for marine insurance and cargoes.

James Wells begins to operate a semi-weekly stage and boat line between Philadelphia and New York with a policy of "load or no load" for departures.

May 25. The College of Philadelphia receives its first entrants.

October 3. Robert Hunter Morris is appointed lieutenant governor following Hamilton's resignation over the embattled issues of paper money and defense of the frontier. Morris encounters conflict with the Quaker-dominated assembly over the question of protecting the province against the Indians and French.

1755    The defeat of General James Braddock stirs popular discontent with Quaker ascendancy in the assembly, and control passes to other Christian sects.

The College Academy and Charitable School, originated by Franklin, is chartered.

Dr. Francis Allison, a Presbyterian clergyman, originates the Ministerial Fund, the first form of life insurance in the United States.

1756    A stage coach line begins runs between Philadelphia and New York.

March. Benjamin Franklin is elected colonel of the Philadelphia regiment, a well-trained outfit prepared to battle the Indians.

August 20. Colonel William Denny arrives as the new governor of Pennsylvania. However, his subservience to the proprietary interest stirs popular disfavor.

December. The first patients are admitted for treatment in the Pennsylvania Hospital.

1757    Businessmen of Philadelphia lobby the assembly to send Benjamin Franklin as a colonial agent to England to express to the Crown the dissatisfaction of the people with proprietary rule.

1759    The Union Library Company is organized by Governor Denny.

The Southwark Theater, the first theater in North America, is opened on South Street.

James Hamilton replaces the unpopular William Denny as governor of the colony.

December 6. Germantown Academy is organized at a meeting of citizens in the home of Daniel Mackinett. It is founded in order to promote the correct use of the English language and teach social accomplishments to young ladies.

1762        Southwark, the oldest outlying district of the city, is created by an act of the assembly.

A medical school is organized by Dr. Shippen. Bodies of suicides are used for the purpose of dissection.

1764        Winter. The Paxton Boys march on Philadelphia to attack Indians kept there for protection from vengeful frontiersmen. However, these angry Scotch-Irish settlers are persuaded by the citizens to return to Lancaster.

1765        May 3. The board of trustees of Philadelphia College approves Dr. John Morgan's plan to add a College of Physicians to the institution. It is the first medical school in the Colonies.

1767        William Goddard founds the city's fourth newspaper, the Pennsylvania Chronicle and Universal Advertiser.

May 20. Philadelphia celebrates the news of the repeal of the Stamp Act. They present gifts to the entire crew of the Minerva which brings the favorable report.

1768        Merchants of Philadelphia meet to protest the British prohibition of steel furnaces at a time when iron products are in great demand in the city.

The first class graduates from the College of Physicians.

Arrangements are made for street cleaning and regular collection of garbage.

1769        David Rittenhouse observes the transit of Venus in an observatory built in the garden behind the State House.

1770          A separate school for black children is opened.

              During the 1770s town pumps are installed out of public funds
              to replace the infested privately operated pumps; the nation's
              first river bridge is erected across the Schuylkill River at
              Market Street.

1771          The Friendly Sons of St. Patrick is organized as a mutual
              benevolent association to help Irish immigrants.

1772          The Society of the Sons of St. George is organized to aid
              Englishmen in distress.

              May 1. The Tammany Society is founded as a social club.
              While it never became the powerful political force that New
              York's Tammany Hall became in the latter part of the nine-
              teenth century, it developed into a patriotic society during
              the War for Independence, and during the Gênet affair it
              evolved into a strongly partisan Republican organization.

1773          The City Tavern is established as a fashionable rival of the
              London Coffee House. Here importers meet at noon to ar-
              range for loans, insurance, and disposal of cargoes.

              December. Captian Ayres of the British ship, the Polly, is
              told by a Philadelphia crowd that he will not be permitted to
              unload any tea in the Quaker City. Without violence, the
              captain obeys and departs from the city.

1774          Paul Revere rides from Boston to Philadelphia to obtain aid
              from the Quaker City in resisting the closing of Boston's
              harbor.

              May 20. A committee of correspondance is organized at the
              City Tavern on Second Street to support the cause of Ameri-
              can liberty against infringements by the British.

              June 1. Businessmen of Philadelphia protest the shutdown
              of the port of Boston by closing their firms for the day.

              June 18. A patriotic mass meeting declares the Boston Port
              Bill unconstitutional and calls for a meeting of a Continental
              Congress.

              September 4. The First Continental Congress meets in Car-
              penter's Hall. It appeals to Great Britain to remove abridge-

ments of colonial rights and declares against any importation of English merchandise.

1775        The United Company of Philadelphia for Promoting American Manufactures is organized.

Pennsylvania Magazine and American Monthly Magazine, the first organ to print the writings of Thomas Paine when he came to Philadelphia, is established by Robert Aitken.

April 25. A mass assembly gathers at the State House in response to news of the battles at Lexington and Concord. Troops are organized to defend the citizens of Philadelphia against attack.

May 5. Benjamin Franklin returns from England to Philadelphia and is elected by the assembly as a delegate to the Continental Congress.

May 10. The Second Continental Congress convenes at Carpenter's Hall.

July 3. The Committee of Safety, organized by Franklin, meets in order to provide Philadelphia and Pennsylvania with a viable civil government. Franklin unanimously is chosen its president.

PHILADELPHIA IN THE AMERICAN REVOLUTION
1776-1781

1776        January 20. The Society of Friends at its annual meeting issues its "Ancient Testimony, " signed by John Pemberton, declaring the loyalty of Quakers to the Crown and their determination to oppose any action for independence.

June 24. The Conference of Pennsylvania adopts a declaration stating its willingness to join in a vote of Congress for independence.

July 4. The Declaration of Independence is adopted by the Continental Congress.

July 8. John Nixon, a famous banker, reads the Declaration of Independence to a jubilant population. Exuberant demonstrations are held throughout the capital city.

July 15. The convention to adopt a new constitution for Pennsylvania meets in Philadelphia. Under Franklin's influence it drafts in the succeeding months a liberal instrument of government, providing for a unicameral legislature and an executive council in place of a governor.

December. General Israel Putnam puts Philadelphia under martial law.

1777 Betsy Ross, a seamstress, sews the flag designed by Francis Hopkinson in her home located at Arch Street, between Second and Third streets.

March 4. Congress returns to the city from Baltimore.

July 4. Mobs storm the houses of Loyalists.

August 26. George Washington marches the Continental Army through Philadelphia on its trip to Brandywine. He is accompanied by Major General Lafayette.

September 26. British troops march into Philadelphia. The officers are billeted in the homes of the leading citizens.

October 4. Washington resists the occupation of Philadelphia in an engagement with new reenforcements at Germantown against the royal army led by General Howe. However, the Americas lose the battle.

1778 United States Magazine, edited by Philip Freneau, is established.

May 8. Sir Henry Clinton arrives in Philadelphia to replace General Howe as the commander of the British forces.

May. Clinton, in response to the involvement of France in the American cause, agrees to exchange prisoners of war with Washington and withdraw his troops from Philadelphia.

June 18. The last British troops evacuate the city.

Summer. Benedict Arnold is placed by Washington in charge of the military government of Philadelphia; the Continental Congress and the State Government return to the city; the city is beset by a severe inflation and shortage of wheat.

July 9. The Articles of Confederation are adopted and signed.

December 1-12. Thomas Paine writes a series of articles in the Pennsylvania Packet, defending the radical state constitution of 1776.

December 5. Silas Deane publishes an attack upon the radical state leaders in the Pennsylvania Packet.

From December 1778 through February 1779, Washington rests in Philadelphia and is displeased with the extravagant festivities and dissipation of the residents.

1779    The College of Philadelphia is transformed by the state legislature into America's first university, the University of Pennsylvania.

January. The Supreme Executive Council of Pennsylvania issues a proclamation against monopolizers and forestallers, who create inflationary prices.

April 5. The Pennsylvania Assembly enacts legislation to curb prices. It orders merchants to accept continental currency and empowers justices of the peace to fix the price and weight of bread.

May 24. A town meeting is held under radical leadership in the State House yard. General Daniel Roberdeau, a merchant, presents a program which would allow the radicals to control the prices on many goods in Philadelphia.

July. The leftist Committee on Prices renews its attack on Robert Morris for charging higher prices on flour than the regulated one.

October 4. A mob of radical militiamen attacks the home of James Wilson, a lawyer, who supported the unpopular conservative, anti-inflationary viewpoint on the currency question. The incident, called the Fort Wilson riot, is quelled when General Joseph Reed, president of the Pennsylvania Supreme Executive Council, supported by the Light Horse Troop, disperses the crowd.

October. Radicals win the elections in the aftermath of popular disgust which follows the Wilson riot.

November 27. The proprietary charter of the College of Philadelphia is revoked by the assembly which suspects its faculty of harboring Tory sympathies. The school is reorganized as the University of the State of Pennsylvania, and the institution is endowed with funds derived from confiscated lands.

Fall. The proprietary rights of the Penn family are abolished by the assembly.

1780     The Bank of Pennsylvania is organized by Robert Morris with the primary purpose of supplying the army with provisions.

February 29. The assembly passes a bill for the gradual emancipation of slaves.

### THE NATION'S LEADING CITY
### 1781-1790

1781     Francis Bailey publishes a radical organ, the Freeman's Journal, which attacks wealthy conservative men like Robert Morris and urges the acceptance of paper money at par.

June 27. Robert Morris takes the oath of office as Superintendent of Finance and establishes the Office of Finance on Front Street.

From November until March 22, 1782, General Washington and his wife take up residence in the Chew House on Third Street, following Cornwallis' surrender at Yorktown. The winter season is celebrated with much festivity.

December 31. The Bank of North America is chartered by Congress as a national bank under the leadership of Robert Morris.

1782     March 1. The Articles of Confederation are promulgated.

1783     America's first sugar refinery is opened by two entrepreneurs, Jacob Morgan and Samuel Miles, on Vine Street.

June. A small band of soldiers from the Pennsylvania Line march on the city to demand immediate receipt of back pay. A force of 1,500 Continental soldiers, dispatched by Washington, force them to return to their homes. Thereafter, the Congress meets in other cities.

1784 The Pennsylvania Society for the Promotion of the Abolition of Slavery and the Relief of Free Negroes Unlawfully Held in Bondage is organized to lobby the legislature to prevent the shipment of blacks out of the state, where they would be sold into slavery. The legislature responds positively.

September 21. The Packet, organized by William Dunlap and David Claypoole, becomes the first daily newspaper in America.

1785 Francis Bailey publishes the first Philadelphia city directory, the first such type of book printed in the United States.

Thomas Pool brings a circus to the city that features horsemanship as its primary attraction.

The Episcopal Academy is founded. Located on Chestnut Street, near Sixth, it becomes one of the city's most prestigious private schools.

Philadelphia Society for Promoting Agriculture, the earliest agricultural organization in America, is established.

September 14. Franklin returns from France, after being absent from Philadelphia for nine years.

1786 Matthew Carey founds the American Museum, a journal that presents excerpts from the leading American and foreign newspapers and magazines.

A prison riot erupts in the Walnut Street Jail to protest the humiliating procedure of forcing convicts with closely shaven heads to work in gangs cleaning and grading the streets.

Philadelphia Dispensary is founded as the first such medical facility in the United States.

John Fitch builds the first steamboat in the world along the Delaware.

Printers strike when their demand for one dollar a day wage is rejected.

June. Delegates of the Protestant Episcopal churches meet in Philadelphia to organize the Protestant Episcopal Church in North America.

1787    Two blacks of Philadelphia, Absalom Jones and Richard Allen, form a mutual benevolent society, the Free African Society.

The Society for the Alleviation of the Miseries of Public Prisons, the first prison reform society in America, is organized under the direction of Rev. William White. It succeeds in convincing the assembly to reform the scandalous condition of the jails.

May 14. The Constitutional Convention convenes and meets until the 17th of September.

1789    The First Presbyterian General Assembly meets.

The employment of convicts on the streets is abolished.

The Quaker ban against the presentation of theatrical entertainment is removed.

March 11. The first city charter is written since the winning of independence. It empowers the taxpayers to elect both the select and common councils. The chief executive officer, the mayor, is prevented from exercising independent authority, while the councils are assigned the functions of levying taxes, determining appropriations, and enacting local ordinances.

### THE NATION'S CAPITAL
### 1790-1800

A school of law is added to the University of Pennsylvania. James Wilson becomes its director.

Dr. Benjamin Rush forms a Society for the Establishment of Sunday Schools to encourage education among the poor.

The first United States census reveals that New York has outstripped Philadelphia as the most populous city in the nation. The Quaker City, with its population of 28,522, ranks second in size.

Gray's Gardens is opened by Samuel Vaughan.

January 6. Southwark Theatre opens under the management of John Henry and Lewis Hallam. It becomes a famous amusement center that is patronized by the leading citizens of the city.

April 17. Benjamin Franklin dies and is buried in Christ Church. The funeral is attended by 20,000 persons.

May 25. A convention that formally organizes the Universalist religion is held in the city.

September. A new constitution is drawn for Pennsylvania to replace the one of 1776. It is patterned upon line similar to those of the other states.

December. The first Congress to assemble following the ratification of the Constitution convenes in Philadelphia.

1791        James Logan bequeaths his collection of over 100,000 books to the Library Company of Philadelphia.

Bishop William White and Dr. Benjamin Rush organize the American Protestant Sunday School Society.

February 25. The Bank of the United States is chartered.

October 31. Philip Freneau, serving as editor, begins publication of the National Gazette, a pro-Jeffersonian journal.

December 12. The first Bank of the United States opens in Philadelphia.

1792        J.B. Ricketts builds a house for circus performances at Twelfth and Market streets.

The Insurance Company of North America is founded to provide marine insurance.

April 9. Philadelphia and Lancaster Turnpike is chartered, providing a sixty-two mile toll road between the two cities.

September. Mint operations for the United States government begin in a building on Seventh Street, near Filbert Street. David Rittenhouse serves as the first director of the mint.

1793        The Chestnut Theater is completed early in the year. Its performances attract national attention.

January 9. A Frenchman, Jean Pierre Blanchard, makes the first baloon ascension in the United States in the presence of President Washington.

March 30. The Bank of Pennsylvania is chartered as a state bank.

Summer. A virulent epidemic of yellow fever ravages Philadelphia. The sanitary conditions and medical facilities of the municipality are completely inadequate for controlling the disease. Approximately 5,000 people die from the scourge.

1794      Charles Willson Peale, the artist, originates a museum in Philadelphia to popularize science.

America's first trade union, the Federal Society of Cordwainers, organizes in Philadelphia.

The first convention for the abolition of slavery meets in the city.

July. Absalom Jones organizes St. Thomas Church, a separate Episcopalian church for blacks.

1795      Construction is completed on the Lancaster Pike, a toll road that is the largest public work of any type in the United States. Built at the cost of $500,000, it is America's longest well-paved highway.

1796      Philadelphia is the first city to experiment with the use of illuminating gas. It is employed at first solely for decorative purposes at Arch and Third streets.

September 12. Bethel African Methodist Episcopal Church is incorporated under the leadership of Richard Allen. Instituted to protest discrimination suffered by blacks in integrated churches, it provides separate religious services for black worshippers.

September 17. George Washington issues his Farewell Address and has it published in D.C. Claypoole's Daily Advertiser.

November. Citizen Adet, the French minister, requests Frenchmen residing in Philadelphia to wear the tricolor cockade; his plea is heeded not only by the French, but also by the anti-Federalist partisans in the city.

1797  May 10. The first battleship of the new navy, the United States, is launched at Philadelphia.

August 1-November 1. A yellow fever epidemic strikes the city. One thousand, two hundred and ninety-two people die as the disease runs its course.

1798  May 8. Riots break out between pro-French and pro-British factions on the day proposed by President Adams as a time of fasting and prayer. The mob action is suppressed by the militia.

Summer. Another yellow fever epidemic strikes and although huge numbers of people flee the city, 3, 637 die from the scourge. These annual visitations of disease check migration to Philadelphia.

1799  The first organized strike in America is initiated by the Federal Society of Cordwainers, who win a wage boost after nine weeks.

June. The first pipes are laid for Philadelphia's pioneering water supply system engineered by Benjamin H. Latrobe. Powerful engines are used to pump water into homes, businesses, and other places where it is needed. The poor are supplied with free water from street hydrants. This is the first municipal waterworks in the nation.

December 3. The state capital is moved from Philadelphia to Lancaster.

## BASES OF PHILADELPHIA'S GROWTH
### 1800-1870

1800  The Philadelphia Society for the Free Instruction of Indigent Boys is organized to provide night school instruction for poor youths.

Penn House, occupied by Presidents Washington and Adams, is converted into the Union Hotel when the national capital is removed to Washington, D.C.

October. The first abutment of stone is laid for the Schuylkill Bridge at Market Street.

1801    The first Greek revival building in the city, the Bank of
        Pennsylvania, designed by Benjamin Latrobe, is completed.

        The Philadelphia Chamber of Commerce is organized and
        meets in the City Tavern.

        January. Water is pumped from the new municipal water-
        works into a few private residences. The cost is $5 a year.

        February 19. The Delaware and Chesapeake Canal Company
        is incorporated to improve transportation to the hinterland
        of Philadelphia.

1802    The legislature authorizes Philadelphia County to provide
        tuition for children too poor to pay the normal educational
        fees.

        January. Philadelphia merchants send a memorial to con-
        gress requesting aid against seizure of their cargoes by
        French warships.

1803    The Hewson establishment at Germantown manufactures the
        first calico fabrics in the United States.

        Philadelphia National Bank is chartered with a capital of
        $1,000,000.

        A separate maternity ward is established at Pennsylvania
        Hospital. It is the first such ward in the United States.

        February. The Pennsylvania Society for the Encouragement
        of Useful Arts and Manufactures is reorganized. It launches
        a publicity campaign to encourage industry.

        March 28. A tract to the north of the city is incorporated
        as Northern Liberties.

        March 29. A poor law statute is passed, requiring the fam-
        ily of indigent city dwellers to provide for their support.

        December 15. The Philadelphia Hose Company is organized
        and run by volunteers with a budget of $350. Established to
        improve fire fighting facilities, it replaces the bucket with
        a hose as a means of providing speedier service.

1804    Oliver Evans runs a horseless carriage on Market Street,
        the world's first motor vehicle.

A regular stage line is established from Philadelphia to Pittsburgh. Charging a fare of $20 per passenger, it departs regularly once a week and guarantees a maximum voyage of seven days. It becomes the most important route of travel from the eastern seaboard to New Orleans.

Samuel Wetherill begins the first white lead factory in the United States.

Jefferson sweeps the city in the election of 1804.

1805      The Market Street bridge, spanning the Schuylkill, is formally opened.

Charles Willson Peale founds the Academy of Fine Arts, the first genuine school for art instruction in the United States.

1806      January. The Philadelphia Society for the Encouragement of Domestic Manufactures is organized, and Stephen Girard serves as its first president.

1807      May. The Farmers' and Mechanics' National Bank begins operations on Chestnut Street.

1808      A race track is constructed at Hunting Park.

The Walnut Street Theater is established.

April 8. The Roman Catholic diocese of Pennsylvania is founded.

May 7. The Pennsylvania Bible Society is organized.

July. A Premium Society is created, offering bounties for domestic manufactures of goods previously purchased abroad, thereby aiding Jefferson's Embargo order.

1809      A chain bridge is completed early in the year connecting Philadelphia with Camden.

The City Hotel is opened on Third Street, and it becomes a popular resort.

A society is organized to provide vaccination against smallpox for a fee of $2 a year.

Thomas Leiper completes a pioneer railroad line on Crum Creek.

February 2. The Walnut Street Theater presents its first performance, an equestrian exhibition.

1812          Philadelphia banks purchase federal bonds to aid the financing of the War of 1812.

The Pennsylvania Company for Insurance on Lives and Granting Annuities is chartered. It is the nation's first trust bank and regular life insurance company.

The first anthracite coal is brought to Philadelphia by Colonel Shoemaker. Philadelphians deride the idea at first that such material can serve as fuel, but the firm of White and Hazard use this substance for heating the furnace of their wire mill. Eventually, the city is transformed by the new fuel.

The Academy of Natural Sciences is founded under the leadership of John Speakman. It assembles a large collection of specimens and sponsors geographical explorations. It attracts the attention of eminent scientists.

March 24. The township of Moyamensing is incorporated.

1813          A bridge is constructed across the Schuylkill at Spring Garden Street, providing wagoners with an unbroken route from the northern section of the city to the West.

June 4. Friends' Asylum for the Insane is founded.

1814          March 23. Philadelphia becomes engaged in the building of war ships.

August 26. A great town meeting assembles in the State House yard to organize for the defense of Philadelphia, following the news that Washington had fallen to the British. Many fortifications are built. The Committee of Defense constructs a line of fortifications on the western front of the city

1815          March 22. The district of Spring Garden is created.

April. The Sunday school of the First Presbyterian Church commences classes.

1816    The first separate congregation for black Methodists is founded.

The Philadelphia Saving Fund Society, organized by Condé Raguet, becomes the first savings bank in the United States.

Philadelphia improves its public squares and names them Washington, Franklin, Rittenhouse, and Logan squares.

The Chestnut Street Theater replaces its whale oil lamps with gas light. This step marks the first important initiative in converting the city to a new source of illumination.

January. A new fish market is opened.

April 10. The Second Bank of the United States is chartered by Congress with its location in Philadelphia. The businessmen of this city are a driving force behind the new charter.

1817    The state legislature outlaws horse racing along Philadelphia's streets.

A new chain bridge is erected to replace the old one over the Schuylkill Falls.

1818    Philadelphia adopts a system of public education. Using taxes to construct school buildings, purchase texts, and train teachers, the city establishes a unified district to provide a free, systematic education to needy students.

Fall. John Lancaster is invited to live in Philadelphia in order to set up a model school and train teachers in his new method of inexpensive, mass education.

1819    July 4. A statue of Washington, financed by the Society of Cincinnati, is unveiled. It stands today in front of the Museum of Art.

1820    A prison riot erupts in the Walnut Street jail. It is quelled by Colonel Biddle's marine contingent.

1821    The Philadelphia College of Pharmacy and Science, the first school of pharmacy in the United States, is founded by a group of young men.

1823    March 31. The Pennsylvania Railroad Company is chartered

by the state legislature and authorized to construct a railroad between Philadelphia and Columbia in Lancanster County.

1824        Franklin Institute is founded to honor Benjamin Franklin and
            carry on some of his scientific interests.

            The Historical Society of Pennsylvania is established.
            Housed on Locust Street at Thirteenth, it brings together
            valuable collections of books and manuscripts concerned
            with the history of Pennsylvania.

            Eastern Penitentiary is constructed on Fairmount Avenue.
            Designed on the principle of a wagon wheel, it is one of the
            nation's most elegant prisons.

            Mercantile Library is established.

            March.  Dr. George McClellan obtains a charter for Jeffer-
            son Medical College.  It begins its operations in the old
            Tivoli Theater, but is moved in 1828 to its present site at
            Walnut and Tenth.

            April 15.  Work commences on a canal to connect the Dela-
            ware and Chesapeake.

            September 28.  General Lafayette receives a warm recep-
            tion from the city populace.  Festive balls and dinners are
            held for a week in honor of the hero.

1825        Canal projects are launched to connect the Allegheny and
            Susquehanna rivers with Lake Erie, as well as to join the
            Schuylkill and Deleware rivers.

            July.  Lafayette makes a second visit to the city and receives
            even more acclaim from the populace.

1826        May 3.  The cornerstone is laid on the Philadelphia Arcade
            on the site of the old Carpenter mansion at Chestnut Street.
            Copied after the fashionable arcade near Regent Street in
            London, it presents rows of exclusive shops.

            August 17.  The city's first cemetery is established, thus
            superceding the former practice of burying the dead in church
            burial grounds or in Potter's Field.

1827        The Union Burying Ground, Machpelah Cemetery, and the
            Philanthropic Cemetery sell grave sites at a relatively in-
            expensive price, thereby providing residents with a much
            needed urban improvement.

            The Pennsylvania Horticultural Society is organized with
            Horace Binney as its president.

            Journeymen carpenters, joined by painters and glaziers,
            strike for a ten-hour day.

1828        The Workingmen's party is formed at a meeting in the city
            to obtain political and social equality for laborers.

            The Mechanics' Free Press, the first labor journal, is
            started in Philadelphia.

            May 23. Congressional authorization is secured for a break-
            water near the mouth of the Delaware Bay to protect the
            shipping of Philadelphia merchants.

1830        July. Godey's Lady's Book is founded and immediately be-
            comes a best-seller. It displays the fashions of the day as
            well as the writings of popular authors.

1831        September 30-October 7. A free trade convention meets in
            Philadelphia and adopts a memorial to congress, drafted by
            Albert Gallatin.

            December 26. Stephen Girard, the successful merchant and
            public benefactor, dies. He bequeaths to Philadelphia
            $500,000 for the improvement of the eastern front of the
            city; $116,000 to sundry charitable institutions in the city;
            $2,000,000 for the erection and maintenance of a college
            for the education of poor white male orphans; and the resi-
            due of his fortune to the city for the support of the college,
            reduction of taxes, and improvement of police service.

1832        July 5-October 4. Asiatic cholera ravages the city. Despite
            municipal efforts to enforce sanitary regulations, 2,314 be-
            come afflicted with the disease.

1833        The cornerstone of Girard College is laid.

            Temperance reformers in Philadelphia organize the United
            States Temperance Union.

October 15. The Philadelphia Board of Trade is established.

December. A railroad from Philadelphia to Columbia begins regular operations.

December 4. The American Antislavery Society is established at Philadelphia.

1834　　Wills Eye Hospital is founded.

Portage Railroad is opened, connecting Philadelphia and Pittsburgh by canal and railroad.

The basic school laws for Pennsylvania are enacted. Each ward of the city is authorized to elect three directors.

July 13. A race riot erupts. White citizens attack blacks in various sections of the city. Arsonists set fire to a row of homes occupied by blacks on Eight Street.

July 14. Rioters attempt to renew their violence against black people, but are suppressed by the police.

October 14. An election riot breaks out between Democrats and Whigs in the Southwark and Moyamensing districts. A fire is set, forty houses of blacks are burned, and several persons are killed. The Democratic boss, Joel Barlow Sutherland, is elected.

1835　　The Männerchor Society of Philadelphia, the oldest German singing club in the United States, is founded.

Promoters of the Laurel Hill Cemetery purchase the estate of Joseph Sims as a burial site on magnificently landscaped grounds.

March 21. City councils vote to create a gas works to illuminate the city. A plant is ordered to be built on Market Street, near the Schuylkill.

From the spring of 1835 until the fall of 1836, unskilled workers win a series of strikes for higher wages and a ten-hour day.

Summer. The first regatta on the Schuylkill is held. Thousands cheer the oarsmen.

1836        The Philadelphia Public Ledger is begun as the first impor-
            tant newspaper to sell for a penny a copy.

            The world's first public high school is opened in Philadelphia.

            February 8. The recently created gas works begins opera-
            tions to supply consumers with a new source of illumination.

            February 18. Nicholas Biddle secures a charter for the
            Pennsylvania Bank of the United States to replace the Second
            Bank of the United States.

            October 19. Laurel Hill Cemetery is used for the first time
            as a grave site.

1837        Matthew Carey protests the exploitation of female workers
            laboring in the clothing industry in A Plea for the Poor.

            March-April. Blacks are attacked by the Robert Morris
            Hose Company of the Moyamensing district.

            From November 28 to February 22, 1838, a constitutional
            convention meets at Musical Fund Hall to amend the old
            Constitution of 1790. Blacks are excluded from the fran-
            chise.

1838        The first separate newspaper for black readers, the National
            Reformer, is established. However, it lasts for only a
            short period of time.

            May 14. Pennsylvania Hall at Sixth and Haines streets, an
            elegant structure erected for the free discussion of issues,
            is dedicated in a speech by the abolitionist David Paul Brown.

            May 16. An abolitionist meeting gathers at Pennsylvania
            Hall to hear an address by William Lloyd Garrison. Anti-
            black rioters attack the building.

            May 17. Another crowd gathers to harass abolitionists
            and burns down Pennsylvania Hall.

            October 26. Central High School opens, providing instruc-
            tion to eighty-nine boys.

            December 18. Schuylkill Bank, unable to meet its obligation
            in specie, closes its doors. Its directors are held liable for
            a fraudulent issue of the stock of the Bank of Kentucky.

1841        The election laws are changed to make the office of mayor
            a popularly elected position.

            A new department for the insane is established by the Penn-
            sylvania Hospital. Dr. Thomas A. Kirkbride is appointed
            its director.

            September 4. The Pennsylvania Bank of the United States,
            following its reckless speculations in cotton, is forced to
            close its doors.

1842        America's first suspension bridge to cross a river is con-
            structed across the Schuylkill.

            January. Nicholas Biddle is arrested and charged with con-
            spiracy to defraud the stockholders of the Pennsylvania Bank
            of the United States.

            August. A race riot erupts when blacks, marching in a pro-
            cession of the Moyamensing Temperance Society, are as-
            saulted by whites. In the evening, whites renew their attack,
            burning a black recreation center, Smith's Beneficial Hall,
            and a black church on St. Mary's Street. The next day Irish
            laborers assail black workers. A large body of troops stops
            the disturbance.

1843        The Art Union is begun to promote an appreciation of the
            fine arts and encourage young artists.

            Weavers riot in Kensington when some of their numbers re-
            fuse to join a strike for higher wages. The violence sub-
            sides when the rioters learn that General Cadwalader's bri-
            gade is ready to use force.

1844        The city purchases the Lemon Hill estate for $25,000. This
            property becomes the nucleus of Fairmount Park. The spon-
            sors of this park, claiming that a large recreation area
            would improve the municipal water supply, are able to add
            large tracts which evolve into one of the world's largest
            intra-city parks.

            The Philadelphia School of Design for Women is founded.

            May 3. A meeting is held to organize a Native American
            Association in the predominantly Irish ward of Kensington.
            The assembly is dispersed when a band of Irishmen attack
            the group.

May 6. An Irish fire company fires shots into the Nanny Goat Market where nativists are holding a meeting. Several people are killed, including a boy who was carrying a flag for the Native Americans.

May 7. Native Americans meet in the State House yard and pass resolutions to increase the period of naturalization to twenty-one years and to maintain the reading of the Bible in the public schools. A large procession marches into Kensington and is fired upon from the Irish hose building. The nativists then burn the fire house, and the flames spread, destroying about thirty buildings. Further violence is stopped by the militia.

May 8. Nativists burn and sack more buildings in the Irish section. They destroy St. Michael's Church. Other parts of the city are also attacked by anti-Catholic mobs, who set fire to St. Augustine's Church, a parochial school, and several other edifices. Militia regiments are called in to quell the riot. However, a grand jury later rules in favor of the Native Americans.

July 4. Nativists hold an enormous parade of approximately 4,500 participants. Over 50,000 people watch the impressive spectacle, which displays colorful floats, banners, and flags.

July 5. An angry crowd gathers at the Roman Catholic Church of St. Philip de Neri when rumors circulate that the building is being used as a storehouse for ammunition. A riot is prevented by the dispatch of troops to Queen Street.

July 7. Incensed nativists force Irish soldiers to release a patriot they were holding prisoner. When fresh troops are attacked by ruffians on Queen Street, the soldiers open fire, killing several bystanders. The infuriated mob retaliates, and pitched battles are not brought under control until armed reenforcements arrive.

July 11. The council appropriates $10,000 for the creation of a battalion of artillery, a troop of horses, and a regiment of infantry to control any future mob disorders more effectively.

1845    Construction begins on the Cathedral of St. Peter and St. Paul.

The Adventist Church is organized by followers of the Reverend William Miller.

April 12. A new police law requires the municipality to maintain police units consisting of at least one man for every 150 taxable residents. In case of riot, the sheriff of a county is empowered to call to his aid the forces of other districts and the militia. This system replaces the old "watch" plan.

June 11. An incendiary fire destroys the Academy of Fine Arts on Chestnut Street, a museum that contained a valuable collection of paintings.

1846        May 13. War with Mexico inspires the formation of thirty volunteer companies from Philadelphia.

1847        Girard College is opened to its first class of orphan boys.

The Pennsylvania legislature passes a ten-hour day law in response to the agitation of the Working Men's party.

The American Medical Association is formed at Philadelphia.

August 21. One of the worst fires in Philadelphia's history destroys the sugar refinery of L. Broome and Co. and the brewery of Robert Newlin.

September. The Native American party convenes in Philadelphia.

1848        A charter is obtained by Dr. Constantine Hering for the oldest homeopathic medical school, the Hahnemann Medical College in Philadelphia.

June. Gang wars and incendiary fires erupt between the Franklin Hose Company and the Moyamensing Hose Company.

June 7-9. The Whig convention assembles in the Museum Building.

October 9. A race riot breaks out in the California House, a tavern patronized by blacks. The building is set ablaze by a white mob.

October 10. A mob continues to assault the black populace

and burns a frame house on St. Mary's Street.   Many blacks and whites are killed and wounded in the ensuing violence.

1849          Philadelphia Skating Club and Humane Society is organized.

May 30-September 8.  An outbreak of Asiatic cholera takes 1,012 lives.

1850          The Democratic boss, Thomas B. Florence, gets control of the city.  He renews Joel B. Sutherland's old tactics of extending patronage, mouthing pro-labor slogans, and supporting the fundamental economic interests of the city.

The Spring Garden Institute is founded to provide public lectures on scientific subjects.

The Women's Medical College is founded as the first medical school in the world strictly for female students.  The first class of eight young women graduate one year later.

May 3.  The police force is made more efficient by providing an elected marshall for all the police districts.

July 9.  A disastrous fire destroys many buildings in the Water Street area.  Twenty-eight persons are killed, and 367 buildings are consumed by the blaze.

1851          St. Joseph's College is founded as a school of higher education for Catholics.

December 26.  Musical Fund Hall is consumed in a fire shortly after an elaborate dinner held in honor of Louis Kossuth had adjourned.

1852          Wagner Free Institute of Science is created to provide popular, free scientific lectures.

Jenny Lind sings before an enthusiastic audience.

1853          Dr. Alfred Kennedy founds the Polytechnic College of Pennsylvania to provide students with a technical education.

The Bachelors' Barge Club is founded as a sporting boat club of the Schuylkill Navy.

1854          Hunting Park is presented as a gift to the city by the property owners of the area.

Philadelphia Cricket Club is organized by Dr. S. Weir Mitchell.

The first surface lines of an urban transit network are constructed.

Policemen are required to wear uniforms.

February 2. The City of Philadelphia is enlarged by an act of the state legislature which incorporates much outlying territory. The city is divided into twenty-four wards. The various counties are consolidated into one city.

May. Robert T. Conrad, a Know-Nothing candidate, defeats Richard Vaux, a patrician democrat, in the race for mayor under the new charter. He vigorously enforces the Sabbath laws and appoints Nativists to office. He requires members of the police force to be of American birth.

1855      A local Republican chapter is organized in Philadelphia, largely through the activity of a flour miller, William B. Thomas.

1856      Winter. A separate department for the insane is instituted in Pennsylvania Hospital.

February 22. The American party holds its national convention in Philadelphia.

May. Richard Vaux, a Democrat, wins the mayor's office as a firm opponent of Know-Nothingism. He rides to victory by building a coalition based on the support of firehouse gangs and local bosses.

June 17-19. The Republican party holds its first national convention at Musical Fund Hall.

October 11. The "Killers, " an Irish gang supporting the Democratic party, attacks people parading in a torch-light procession through the city.

October 13. A ruffian gang attacks the Shiffler Hose Company, and when counter-violence ensues, the police arrest the Shifflers.

October 14. When members of the Shiffler Hose Company

are taken into prison vans, hundreds protest the action and
jeer the Irish police. The city is shaken with the threat of
more violence.

1857        Bryant and Stratton Business College is founded.

January 26. The Academy of Music is opened to the public.

May. The cornerstone is laid for Holy Trinity Church, located on Walnut and Nineteenth streets.

May. The Philadelphia and Delaware River Railroad Company is empowered to lay tracts for a street railway on
Fifth and Sixth streets. The fare is to be 5 cents.

August 1. The Philadelphia Press, edited by John Wein Forney, prints it first folio. Forney converts the journal from
an ardent pro-Buchanan organ to a vehicle for Republican
opinion.

September 25. The Bank of Pennsylvania closes in a financial panic that sweeps the nation.

1858        The city council passes an ordinance removing market sheds
from Market Street, a practice that had been a nuisance to
other types of business.

January 21. The first street passenger railway line is run
by the Fifth and Sixth Streets Company from Cherry Street
in Kensington to Morris Street in Southwark.

Spring. Richard Vaux is defeated in his bid for reelection
as mayor by Alexander Henry, a Whig, who runs on a platform of opposition to foreign indigents and blacks.

May 7. The Shiffler Hose Company is attacked by a rival
fire company from the Moyamensing district. Although many
shots are fired, nobody is hurt.

May 24. A riot erupts when a policeman tries to arrest a
member of the Lafayette Rifles. The mob sides with the police when one of them is struck by a soldier, and other members of his company prevent his arrest. Several people are
killed.

July 3. Mayor Henry is arrested on the complaint of an officer of the Board of Health for refusing to close down a police station.

July 6. Mayor Henry is acquitted in court of the charge of defying an officer of the Board of Health.

1859        April 4. A case involving an alleged runaway slave, Daniel Dangerfield, is brought before a Philadelphia court under the Fugitive Slave Act. The black is released.

December 7. A meeting sponsored by merchants who were carrying on a lucrative trade with the South condemns John Brown's raid at Harper's Ferry.

1860        January 14. Local forces are brought together for the formation of the Constitutional Union party at the Academy of Music.

February 20. The Continental Hotel, the largest hostelry in the United States, is opened to the public. Many distinguished guests, including the first Japanese embassy to the nation, visit it.

March. A black mob tries to rescue Moses Horner from being returned to his Southern owner.

November. Philadelphia gives Lincoln a majority of more than 2,000 votes over all three of his rivals in the national election for the presidency.

1861        February 21-22. Abraham Lincoln, as President-elect, visits the city and receives an enthusiastic reception.

April-May. Philadelphia takes a stand of ardent loyalty to the Union and raises eight regiments to serve the national cause.

May. Jay Cooke, a Philadelphia financier, sells government bonds to raise money for creating and equipping the Pennsylvania reserve. He sells the entire issue within two weeks.

1862        League Island is purchased by the city.

April 20. Religious services are inaugurated in the Cathedral of St. Peter and Paul.

December 27. The Union League of Philadelphia is created to aid in the successful prosecution of the war. The city generally exhibits more loyalty to the nation during the war than New York City.

1863        La Salle College, a Catholic institution, is founded.

An epidemic of scarlet fever ravages the city.

June. A special meeting of the city council gives the mayor $500,000 to be spent for the defense of the state.

June 29. Governor Curtin and Mayor Henry urge all able-bodied men to volunteer for emergency military service to defend the city against attack.

July 1. Most business establishments are closed as men go to fight the Confederacy, following fears raised by the Battle of Gettysburg.

1864        June 7. Philadelphia hosts the Council Fair of the Sanitary Commissions from Pennsylvania, New Jersey, and Delaware in Logan Square.

November 20. The Cathedral of St. Peter and Paul is consecrated.

1865        February 8. A destructive fire erupts in a coal-oil factory on Ninth Street, causing severe loss of lives and property.

April 3. News of the fall of Richmond to the Union army sparks spontaneous demonstrations and celebrations of tumultuous joy throughout the city.

April 22. The city mourns the assassination of Abraham Lincoln. Thousands visit his hearse, which is brought to lay in state in Independence Hall.

April 30. A plot to burn the city is discovered and foiled by General Cadwalader. The municipal authorities adopt strong defensive measures to prevent any new incendiary attempts.

July 22. Volunteer soldiers from New York create a riot when the Philadelphia police attempt to arrest them for disorderly conduct. They attack many citizens while drunk and elude arrest.

October 10. Morton McMichael of the Union party is elected mayor.

October 17. The Philadelphia Fire Department holds an impressive parade and jubilee. The eighty-four companies display their steam engines, hose carriages, and ambulance They are joined by thirty visiting fire companies from other cities.

1866        June 23. Chestnut Street Bridge is completed. Its opening ushers in a period of westward expansion of the city.

July-November. Another scourge of cholera hits the city.

August 14. A convention of Johnson Republicans meets in Philadelphia. Many inhabitants of the city are infuriated by the fraternization of Unionists with former Confederates.

1867        March 22. Blacks are granted the right to ride on street cars in Philadelphia.

June 17. The Philadelphia Corporation declines to welcome President Johnson.

June 26. George W. Childs builds the first newspaper edifice in the nation. It houses his publication, the Public Ledger.

1868        Daniel M. Fox, a Democrat, is elected mayor in a contest alleged to be marked with much fraudulent voting.

Mary 1. Democrats stage a mass meeting to protest the impeachment of President Johnson.

1869        June 1. Dr. James Rush bequeaths his estate to the Philadelphia Library Company. The money is to be used to build a new fireproof home and to maintain the library.

July 7. The Supreme Court of Pennsylvania upholds the Philadelphia Registry Law of 1868, passed to secure honest elections by limiting the franchise to qualified registered voters.

August 16. The National Labor Union convention meets in the city.

PHILADELPHIA AS A COSMOPOLITAN AND EXPANDING CITY
1870-1915

1870            The Record is published for the first time.

Blacks demonstrate in celebration of the adoption of the Fifteenth Amendment.

1871            A paid professional fire department replaces the volunteer hose companies.

William S. Stokley, a man who gains popularity from his fight against the gas trust and volunteer fire companies, is elected mayor. He strengthens the police department, but allows bossism and corruption to flourish.

Work is begun on the erection of a new City Hall.

The Philadelphia Board of Surveyors is empowered to plan for the future development of the municipality.

Summer. The Citizens' Municipal Reform Association is organized as a bi-partisan effort to purge both the Republican and Democratic parties of corrupt rings and to bring to office men of high integrity.

October. Anti-black riots, sparked by the enfranchisement of the blacks, erupt in the Fourth and Fifth wards. Two prominent blacks, Professor Octavius Catto and Isaiah Chase, are killed. The militia is summoned to restore order.

December 8. The City Treasury suspends operations following discovery of fraud and misappropriation of funds within the department.

1872            February 27. Party officials are tried in court for election fraud.

June 5. The national Republican convention opens its session at the Academy of Music.

October. Ruffians are employed to intimidate those who seek to reform the city of corrupt rule in an election campaign marked by violence.

November. The Citizens' Municipal Reform Association succeeds in brining to public light the defalcations of the city treasurer and in exerting pressure for his conviction.

December 7. The cornerstone is laid for a new building to house the Academy of Fine Arts on Broad and Cherry streets.

1873    September 18. A financial panic, which sweeps the country, begins with the failure in Philadelphia of E. W. Clarke and Company, and in New York City of Jay Cooke and Company.

September 26. A new Masonic Temple, located at Filbert and Broad streets, is dedicated.

October. Reformers challenge the ring by putting up a ticket of candidates with irreproachable reputations.

1874    February 6. Franklin Savings Fund, a bank which had attracted deposits from working class people, goes bankrupt. Labor unrest and strikes follow the ensuing depression.

March 15. A Sunday Liquor Law is passed.

July 4. The cornerstone is laid for a new City Hall in Penn Square; ground is broken in West Fairmount Park for the Centennial Exhibition; the Girard Avenue bridge, constructed at the cost of almost $1,500,000, is opened.

July 14. A cornerstone is laid for a building to commemorate the centennial of American independence.

December 23. An ordinance is passed by the council reorganizing the Highway Department.

1875    Belmont Driving Association lays out a magnificent race track at Cynwyd.

1876    The School of Industrial Art is founded, thanks to the leadership of Mrs. E. D. Gillespie.

April 22. The new home for the Academy of Fine Arts is opened to the public.

May 10. The Centennial Exposition to honor the founding of the nation is opened to the public. It uses a World's Fair format, exhibiting the products and inventions of many countries. It emphasizes the progress that has been made by the United States in its one hundred years of independence.

1877      Robert E. Pattison, a reformer, is elected on the Democratic ticket to the post of Controller. His investigations reveal the corrupt finances of the Republican machine.

June 2. A commission investigates corruption in the customs house.

July 23. A strike by the Pennsylvania Railroad employees triggers riots in Philadelphia, which are quelled quickly by the police.

August 11. The Working Men's Protective Party organizes as a new third party in Caledonian Hall. Formed largely through the efforts of the Typographical Union, the delegates express an essentially conservative purpose of using the power of labor to exert pressure on politicians to enact laws which will protect the working class.

September 12. The Democratic nominating convention meets in the city.

November 6. A new project of docks and warehouses is launched.

1878      John Wanamaker transforms the illumination of his store by using electricity, the first such experiment in merchandising in America.

The Bell Company establishes its first downtown offices in the city on Chestnut Street. Before long, the telephone becomes an integral part of city life.

February 13. Mrs. Sarah Harrison presents to the Academy of Fine Arts a distinguished collection of paintings.

June 11. The Working Men's party holds a mass meeting.

August 13. The National Greenback-Labor convention meets.

August 22. Fraud is discovered in the Water Bureau.

1879      February 12. A black is admitted to a normal school in the city.

October 1. An elevated railroad is constructed on Filbert Street.

December 3. A Democratic convention to select candidates for ward officers and to nominate delegates to attend the state convention is disrupted by fighting among the rival factions. "Squire" Bill McMullen and his gang use armed violence to seat the supporters of the Randall-Tilden ticket. Many riots break out in the city, and a large number of people are wounded.

1880            August 23. A small-pox epidemic breaks out in the slum district of the Fourth Ward.

October 2. George W. Childs and Anthony J. Drexel plan suburban villas in Wayne Station.

December 3. The Committee of One Hundred, respectable businessmen interested in clean government, meet to oust the corrupt machine headed by Mayor Stokley.

December 14. An investigation of the gas trust is held.

December 16. Sophomores and medical students at the University of Pennsylvania riot, and the police are almost overpowered in their efforts to restore order. Ten students are arrested, and three policemen are sent to the hospital with injuries.

1881            February. Reformers succeed in electing Samuel G. King, a Democrat, as mayor.

May 15. Catholic children are withdrawn from public schools on the order of Father Barry.

June 4. A church for the poor is funded in the will of Fannie Smith.

July 26. Citizens agitate for a 5-cent streetcar fare.

December 1. Fraud is discovered in the operation of the almshouses. Members of the Board of Guardians of the Poor are found to have taken public funds and supplies for their own use.

1882            The Brush Electric Light Company, in a campaign to per-

suade the city council to adopt electricity for municipal
lighting, offers to illuminate Chestnut Street for one year
free of charge.  Both the Public Ledger and the Record
switch to electric lighting.

February 9.  Scandal comes to light, revealing the use of
bribery in the contract for the construction of the elevated
railroad.

June 29.  A German choral society holds a Sängerfest.

August 28.  Seventy-five representatives of the Labor Convention meet and resolve to endorse candidates in any party
who favor the interests of workingmen.  They nominate
Thomas A. Armstrong for governor.

September 14.  Election frauds are discovered in the Fourth
Ward.  Lanergan and Johnson are arraigned.

October.  The bi-centennial celebration of the landing of
William Penn is commemorated.  A cheering throng gathers
to witness a spectacle of parades, flags, and the ringing of
the State House bell.

Robert E. Pattison, a reform mayor of the city, is elected
governor.

December 3.  The first street electric light in Philadelphia
is turned on by the Brush Company.

1883            The bi-centennial of the founding of Germantown is celebrated.

April 7.  Cable street cars, operated by electricity, are
opened along a mile-long track from Twenty-third Street to
Fairmount Park.  The cars travel twice the speed of horse-
drawn carriages.

1884            Temple University is founded by a Baptist minister, Dr.
Russell H. Conwell, as a means of helping economically dis-
advantaged youths to attain a higher education.

Mid-summer.  Over 6,000 people are thrown out of work
by the closing of the cotton and woolen mills in Manayunk,
an important manufacturing suburb.  Employees in saw
mills, ship yards, and foundries also lose their jobs.

November. The Philadelphia Tribune, a black weekly, is
established by Christopher J. Perry.

December 18. The South Mountain Water Company is
chartered.

1885     June 1. The Bullitt Act is passed by the Pennsylvania legislature. It gives the city a new charter which reduces the
number of municipal departments from twenty-eight to eight
and places them under the direct control of the mayor.

July 19. Water impurities from the Schuylkill River are discovered.

1886     September 22. Drunken policemen terrify the populace in
the Fifth Ward when they shoot and club peaceful citizens.

1887     A Republican, Edwin H. Fitler, is elected mayor under the
new charter, and he appoints William Stokley as the director of public safety.

April 1. The Bullitt Act goes into effect, fulfilling the program of the Committee of One Hundred. This new charter
increases the power of the mayor and extends his term of
office to four years.

May. Stricter laws are enacted for the sale of alcoholic
beverages. As a result, the number of saloons in Philadelphia declines.

November 20. A coal strike in Lehigh causes fuel shortages.

1889     December 7. The Art Club of Philadelphia meets for the
first time in an elegant new clubhouse on Broad Street. A
structure that reflects a new awareness for municipal beautification, it is the product of a design competition among
architects of the city.

December 29. An eight-hour law is revived in city departments.

1890     The first country club in Philadelphia is founded by John C.
Bullitt on sixy acres of rolling land.

April 30. A financial panic disrupts the business community,
when numerous banks suspend payments.

September 25. The Democratic party holds its convention.

December 1. A run begins on the Keystone National Bank, a bank which has been the depository of city funds.

December 18. A franchise is granted to the Belt Line Railroad.

**1891**     Edwin S. Stuart, the Republican nominee, defeats the Democratic contender, Albert H. Ladner, in the race for mayor.

March 20. The Keystone National Bank is closed, following revelation of the fraudulent practices used by its officers and City Treasurer John Bardsley.

May 14. The Bourse is organized by businessmen of the city, who each contribute $1,000 toward its capital stock of $1,000,000.

May 21. John Bardsley, treasurer of the city, resigns because of his role in misappropriating public funds. He later is sentenced to prison.

December 17. The Drexel Institute of Art, Science and Industry is formally dedicated.

**1892**     The University of Pennsylvania opens its graduate school to women students.

April 27. Six people are killed in a fire in the Grand Central Theatre.

A trolley car is opened on Catherine and Bainbridge Streets.

**1893**     January 29. The Reading Terminal is opened on Twelfth and Market streets, extending railway service to the Main Line.

July 16. The Walnut Street bridge is formally opened to the public.

**1894**     Broad Street is paved with asphalt.

January 25. The National Conference for Good City Government meets to exchange ideas on ways to cleanse municipal politics and to work toward electing men of recognized ability and high integrity.

July 12. The local lodges of Orangemen are attacked by a gang of green-ribbon men when they parade down Broad Street. The rioters are clubbed by the reserves, and many are sent to Hahnemann Hospital.

December 29. The Municipal League revolts against Matthew Quay's and Boies Penrose's corrupt control of politics. They organize to elect an honest man as mayor.

1895    Various independent street line companies are consolidated into the Union Traction Company. It, in turn, is subsequently absorbed by the Philadelphia Rapid Transit Company.

Dr. William E.B. DuBois comes to Philadelphia to research the history of the black population of the city.

Compulsory education is instituted for all children in the city.

February 20. Charles F. Warwick is elected mayor, defeating "Boss" David Martin, the municipal henchman of the Quay machine.

February 22. The Free Library of Philadelphia is opened.

May 28. A mass meeting is held at the Academy of Music to promote the principle of sound money. A Sound Money League is organized to agitate for a single gold standard.

September 2. A riot breaks out on Labor Day when two Italian Socialists wave a red flag during a parade. Law enforcement officials are hooted by a mob when they attempt to arrest the men.

December 21. A mob of about 200 people attack a railway car of the Union Traction Company in protest over the dismissal of 1,000 workers who had been on strike.

December 30. The Philadelphia Bourse is formally opened.

1896    City Hall, the largest contemporary building in America, is completed. It stands on the intersection of Broad and Market streets.

February 23. Captain John Hart is convicted for launching a filibustering expedition to Cuba from Philadelphia.

May. The bankrupt Philadelphia and Reading Company and the Philadelphia and Reading Coal and Iron Company are sold to J.P. Morgan and Company.

1897

June 2. President McKinley opens the Commerical Museum.

October 11. Irish and American women, employed in Campbells' cotton mill, attack three young Russian Jewesses to protest the hiring of foreigners in the factory. The police intervene, promising to protect the Jewish girls when they return to their jobs.

December 23. Chestnut Street National Bank fails.

1898

March 25. The People's Bank of Philadelphia closes following disclosures of fraud and misappropriations of city funds.

October 25. President William McKinley attends the city's Peace Jubilee, held to commemorate the conclusion of the Spanish-American War.

1899

Jules Junker, a businessman, brings the first motor car to the city from France.

Philadelphia College of Osteopathy is established under the leadership of Dr. O.J. Snyder and Mason W. Priestly.

June 30. The mayor and other municipal dignitaries ride in the first passenger train to run over the entire length of the new subway.

October 6. The Philadelphia Electric Company is incorporated with an authorized capital of $25,000,000.

December 7. P.A.B. Widener purchases thirty-six acres of land, on which he later establishes the Widener Industrial Home for Crippled Children.

1900

The Philadelphia Orchestra is founded.

May. Gimbel Brothers purchase the Girard House at Ninth and Chestnut streets as a site for an annex to their department store.

June 19-21. McKinley is nominated for the presidency in a national convention held in the city.

1901            January 8.  A crusade is launched against vice under the
                leadership of Bishop Potter.

                March.  A new Gray's Ferry Bridge is opened.

1902            The Philadelphia Rapid Transit Company is chartered.

                Theodore Roosevelt dedicates a new Central High School at
                Broad and Green streets.

                The Automat is introduced as a new concept in commercial
                dining.

                June 20.  A school bribery scandal is uncovered.

1903            February 17.  John Weaver is elected mayor.  He pledges
                to drive the gamblers out of the city.

1904            A drive for pure meat is launched.

                Lincoln Steffen's Shame of the Cities is published, exposing
                the corrupt practices of Philadelphia's Republican political
                machine.

1905            The city council agrees to build the Fairmount Parkway bou-
                levard, to connect the new museum of art with City Hall.

                A new school law is passed by the Pennsylvania legislature
                that creates a modern, centralized, bureaucratic system.
                Power is taken from decentralized school boards in the va-
                rious wards of Philadelphia and placed in a Board of Educa-
                tion, headed by a powerful superintendent of schools.

                February 10.  A crusade is launched against police corrup-
                tion.

                February 23.  Subway plans are completed for a City Hall
                extension.

                May 24.  A typhoid epidemic plagues the city.

                May 26.  Mass meetings are staged to assail the Republican
                ring that controls city politics.

1906            March 15.  The Philadelphia and Western Railroad Company
                plans to construct an elevated railroad and subway.

1907     The park system is extended by the additions of Pennypacker and Cobbs parks.

February. The Republican organization triumphs in the mayoralty campaign, putting into office its candidate, John E. Reyburn.

March 4. The Market Street Subway is opened.

July 1. The city signs its first contract with the Philadelphia Rapid Transit Company.

July 23. The Poor Richard Club is organized.

1908     Oscar Hammerstein's Philadelphia Opera House is opened with a performance of Bizet's Carmen.

The Y.M.C.A. Building on Arch Street is dedicated.

April. Shibe Park is opened as a home for the Philadelphia American League baseball club.

August 4. The new city subway is opened to the public.

1909     Regular passenger service is launched on the new elevated tracks of the Philadelphia and Reading Railroad.

A thirty-five foot channel of the Delaware is approved by the War Department, thus allowing Philadelphia to compete with the world's great seaports.

February 19. A new system of water works is put into use.

May. Transit workers of the Philadelphia Rapid Transit Company strike for higher wages.

May 28. The council decides to provide a widened parkway for the city.

June. A gas engine apparatus is installed in a new fire pumping station.

June. Transit workers strike, and a riot ensues.

December 20. Seven thousand women shirtwaist makers go on strike, partially in response to a similar protest in New

York. The women succeed in securing improved working
conditions.

1910        The first airplane flight from New York to Philadelphia is
sponsored by the New York Times and the Philadelphia Public Ledger.

The Aquarium in Fairmount Park is completed.

The Historical Society of Pennsylvania moves to a new home
at Thirteenth and Locust streets.

February 19. The Amalgamated Association calls a strike
of trolley men, thus paralyzing the city. Violence and disorder mark the work action.

February 23. Rioting, involving striking transit workers,
is brought under control when the state's mounted constabu-
lary is brought into the city.

March 7. The Central Labor Union calls a general strike
in sympathy for the transit workers. Sixty thousand men
in seventy-five unions support the order, but the strike nevertheless is defeated by the intervention of state troopers.

1911        The independent reform candidate for mayor, Rudolph Blankenburg, beats the Republican machine controlled by Boies
Penrose. He discontinues the corrupt practices of his pre-
decessors, who had made huge profits on street maintenance
and utility contracts. He brings an efficient, non-partisan
administration to the city.

1913        Militant feminists, led by Mrs. Lucretia Blankenburg,
campaign for the right to vote.

May. Longshoremen strike and are enflamed by I.W.W.
agitators.

December. The establishment of a new art museum is announced.

1914        During World War I, 1914-1918, Philadelphia becomes an
"arsenal of democracy, " converting its industries to war-
time needs. It furnishes 40 percent of American military
commodities supplied to the Allied troops and the United
States during World War I.

February. A slight earthquake jolts the city.

December. A large percentage of Philadelphia's wage earners face the prospect of unemployment.

## PHILADELPHIA AS A METROPOLITAN CENTER
## 1915-1970

1915

"Jitney" bus service in private cars becomes a rage, until they are forced out of business by the traction interests.

April. A curfew for children under fifteen years of age is instituted.

June 15. Mayor Blankenburg authorizes the Department of Wharves, Docks and Ferries to acquire property for ten municipal piers in the Moyamensing district.

July 25. An Italian mob disrupts a socialist meeting called to protect reservists from returning to military duty.

November 2. The regular Republican organization returns to power with the election of Thomas B. Smith as mayor.

1916

July. Members of the International Association of Machinists go on strike.

August 6. The Amalgamated Association of Street and Electric Railways calls a strike for higher wages.

August. New traffic regulations are instituted.

1917

April. Philadelphia mobilizes her resources for the war effort when the United States becomes actively involved in the conflict. Her citizens readily purchase war bonds. One of her most important contributions is the construction of war ships.

April 10. An explosion at the Eddystone Ammunition Works kills many Philadelphians and demolishes numerous homes.

May 1. The first war contract for rifles for the American army is granted to the Remington Arms Company.

September 15. Work is begun on a ship yard at Hog Island to aid the war effort.

September 19. A policeman, George Eppley, is murdered
during a primary election, as a result of a political feud.
The mayor, a councilman, and a police lieutenant are indicted later on charges of conspiracy.

November 9. The Philadelphia Orchestra Association bans
German music from its programs.

December 4. A pro-German saboteur is discovered in the
Frankford Arsenal.

December 19. Mayor Thomas B. Smith is indicted by a
grand jury for conspiring to violate the election law by hiring a gunman to kill policeman Eppley in the Fifth Ward.

1918        April 20. The federal government takes over the police department to aid in an antivice campaign.

July 28. Racial tensions generate riots in the city.

September 26. Mayor Smith is issued a warrant for arrest
on charges of misconduct in office. He is accused of forcing
the appointment of a corrupt supervisor of recreation.

1919        From 1919 to 1929, the central part of the city is rebuilt
with new skyscrapers, transforming the appearance of the
city.

A new municipal charter is passed, authorizing the establishment of a regular planning commission.

January. Mayor Smith is acquitted of charges of misconduct
in office.

May 12. One million dollars is left as a trust fund by T. S.
Harrison for use in improving municipal conditions.

April 23. Two Communists attack a government agency on
a U.S. pier, and are nearly killed by laborers.

November 1. The Constitutional Liberty League plans to
test the blue law by holding a baseball game on Sunday.

November 4. J.H. Moore is elected mayor.

1920        January 5. The two city councils are merged into one, and
the number of councilmen is reduced.

June 18. Two men are shot during a dispute over a longshoremen's strike. Ammunition is discovered in the I.W.W. building.

September 25. C.H.K. Curtis buys the Philadelphia Press.

1921     Edward Bok, editor of the Ladies' Home Journal, sets up a trust fund to present the Philadelphia Award as a stimulus to civic improvement.

January 18. The Councils Finance Commission appropriates $10,000 to set up a municipal clearing house to relieve the hardships of the unemployed.

March 6. Radicals are arrested.

March 28. Philadelphia Quakers request President Harding to initiate a world disarmament meeting.

April 7. The city stages an Americanization rally and parade to commemorate United States entry into World War I.

April. The Philadelphia Rapid Transit Company cuts wages.

December 1. Philadelphia General Hospital opens a radium clinic for the treatment of cancer.

1922     February 7. The Philadelphia Dress and Waist Manufacturers Association is threatened with a $1,000,000 suit by the International Ladies' Garment Workers' Union for conspiracy to destroy the union.

November 5. The Market Street subway is extended to Frankford Avenue and Bridge Street to facilitate mass transit to the northeast quarter of the city.

December 1. J.R. Shoemaker, local organizer of the Ku Klux Klan, challenges a police order against staging a parade.

1923     May 14. The annual survey of the Philadelphia Housing Association reveals a housing shortage and exorbitant rents.

November 7. The regular Republican machine candidate, W.F. Kendrick, wins the race for mayor.

December 20. A proposal is made to reform the police department, along lines similar to that of the army.

1924        January 5. Mayor-elect Kendrick promises a quick campaign to clear the city of vice.

January 8. The Director of Public Safety, Brigadier General Smedley Butler, orders undesirables to leave Philadelphia. Police barriers are raised in New York and Baltimore.

January 11. Nine hundred and seventy-three saloons are closed. Brigadier General Butler threatens severe penalties against reckless drivers.

January 15. Six hundred policemen are transferred from desk jobs to the beat. Butler seeks increases in the salary of policemen and a reduction of the number of men on the force.

January 16. Firemen are armed and used as auxillary policemen.

January 22. The Civil Service Commission approves Butler's merit promotion proposal.

January 31. The Civil Service Commission grants Butler full disciplinary powers over the police force.

February 3. A medical emergency corps is organized to combat disease.

May 11. The Curtis Institute of Music is started by Mary Louise Bok, wife of the celebrated editor. A tuition-free school, it attracts eminent musical talents to its faculty like Leopold Stokowski.

May 15. The beautification of Independence Square is planned.

August. Work is begun on the North Broad Street subway.

September. The Philadelphia Civic Grand Opera Company plans to perform the city's first civic opera supported entirely by public funds.

September 29. The Law Enforcement League organizes a mass meeting to prevent Mayor Kendrick from ousting Butler as Director of Public Safety.

October 16.  The quarrel between Butler and Kendrick is patched up.  Butler retains his post as head of the police force.

1925      January.    A site is chosen for a new athletic stadium.

September 20.  A drive is launched by public schools to immunize children against scarlet fever and diphtheria.

October 30.  Mayor Kendrick meets with President Coolidge to request an extension of the leave for Brigadier General Butler from the Marine Corps so that he can continue his drive against prohibition violators.  Coolidge refuses on November 4.

November 16.  Nineteen election board officials are indicted by a grand jury for fraud.

December 27.  Butler is replaced on his post by G.W. Elliott. The ousted Butler calls Philadelphia a "cesspool of vice" and blames Kendrick for the corruption.  He asserts that big hotels violate the dry laws.  Governor Pinchot praises his work.

December 29.  Hotels suffer loss of clientele for New Year's Eve celebrations in the wake of a drive to enforce the prohibition laws.  The Philadelphia Law Enforcement League and women's organizations criticize the dismissal of Butler.

1926      February 27.  The police arrest 1,000 undesirables.  The new Director of Public Safety continues the drive against vice.

July 1.  Delaware Bridge is opened, connecting Philadelphia and Camden.

July 4.  A world exposition is opened to celebrate the sesquicentennial of the signing of the Declaration of Independence.  Controversy erupts over the Sunday opening of the fair.

1927      February 2.  The city council launches a $20,000,000 beautification program.

May 5.  Franklin Institute is offered a parkway plot as a site for a new $4,000,000 museum.

November 8. Mackey wins the contest for mayor in an election marked with charges of fraud.

1928            The North Broad Street Subway is opened.

November 25. The chairman of the Committee of Seventy canvasses public opinion on the proposal to replace the mayor with a city manager.

December 3. Plans are formulated for an airport terminal.

1929            March 2. A movement is begun to adopt a city manager plan of municipal government.

September.    Vare Republicans sweep most of the wards in a hotly contested primary election.

November.    Plans are made for a new municipal art center.

1930            May.    The Philadelphia Society for the Preservation of Landmarks is organized.

May 18. An elevated express highway is planned by the Philadelphia Board of Trade.

1931            November.    The Vare machine Republican candidate, J.H. Moore, wins the race for mayor.

December 16. The city treasury is declared bankrupt. Banks refuse to float loans. Twenty-five thousand municipal employees fail to receive their salaries.

December 20. Salary cuts of municipal employees are planned, to cope with the fiscal crisis.

1932            February 14. The Pennsylvania Regional Planning Federation creates a plan for a Philadelphia Tri-State District to include areas of Pennsylvania, New Jersey, and Delaware.

April 4. One thousand, five hundred and seventy-one municipal employees are dismissed in an economy drive.

December 22. The city achieves a balanced budget by cutting the salaries of its employees.

1933    January 2. The Bureau of Municipal Research reports a $12,000,000 budget deficit.

       June 20. Mayor Moore rejects the initiative of civic leaders to secure $100,000,000 in federal funds.

       November 7. A coalition of Democrats and Republicans defeat the Vare machine.

1934    South Broad Street and Ridge Avenue Connector subway is begun to improve mass transit.

       April 9. The Philadelphia Inquirer merges with the Philadelphia Public Ledger. Both names are used in the masthead of the newspaper.

       June. An agreement is reached to cooperate with police forces within a fifty mile radius of the city. The new regional law enforcement agency is to serve as an integral unit.

       June 21. The Philadelphia Council approves a pact with the Delaware River Joint Bridge Commission to create a high speed line.

1935    January 3. Reverend F.D. Getty assails the city for its callousness to the poor and its failure to appropriate sufficient sums to provide welfare for the underprivileged.

       February 9. Several members of the police department are suspended for taking bribes from drunken drivers and then placing these pay-offs into the policeman's pension fund.

       February 17. Mayor Moore claims that the city's credit has dried up. He refuses to borrow more money for unemployment aid.

       November 5. The Republican candidate, S.D. Wilson, wins the hotly contested mayoralty election. The victory is interpreted as a rebuff of the New Deal.

1936    February 13. The city council passes an ordinance requiring all criminals in the city to be registered.

       May 24. The Philadelphia Central Labor Union sets up a ward organization in order to participate in politics.

June. The Democratic party holds its national convention in Philadelphia.

August 14. The police department is shaken up amidst reports of collusion in vice and gambling facilities.

November 4. The city votes for the Democrats in the national election.

December 28. Plans for city control of elevated, subway, and bus lines win court approval. The city hopes to create a 5-cent fare.

December. A wageless pay day is feared for municipal employees. Controller White decries any schemes that will lead to further imbalances in the budget.

1937        July 8. The council approves taxes on savings and insurance companies, in order to increase municipal revenues.

November 3. The Democrats win at the polls in the wake of Mayor Wilson's defection from the Republican party.

1938        January 27. The council votes sales, billboard, and lubrication oil taxes in an effort to secure additional revenues.

February. Mayor Wilson, in response to labor pressure, vetoes the tax bill.

March 3. The new tax package is upheld in the courts.

March 6. The new taxes go into effect.

August 20. Prisoners go on a hunger strike to protest their inadequate diet.

August 27. Prison conditions arouse protest by citizens in the wake of public disclosure that four men died from heat in isolation cells.

November. An ordinance is signed requiring residents to pay a 1/2 percent income tax.

December. The State Supreme Court upholds the new income tax law.

1939      August 11. Mayor Wilson resigns because of illness, and he is replaced by the city council president, G. Connell.

August 27. The Muncipal Research Bureau urges the consolidation of city and county governments.

November 7. Republicans maintain control of the city's administration. Their candidate, Lamberton, defeats R.C. White in the race for mayor. The vote indicates that blacks have shifted their allegiance to the Republican party.

1940      January 12. The city income tax is upheld in a test case brought by the ILGWU against the Waist and Dress Manufacturer's Association for deducting this money from the payroll of its employees.

March 7. The city council approves a loan to improve the water and sewer system.

1941      July 19. The state legislature kills three charter reform bills.

1942      September 16. The State, County and Municipal Employees American Federation agrees to a compromise wage offer, which averts a strike.

1943      July 3. A city-wide curfew is recommended by a grand jury in order to combat juvenile delinquency.

November 2. Mayor B. Samuel, a Republican, wins his election bid with a large majority.

1944      January 11. A strike by street cleaners for higher wages leaves the city with mounting piles of litter.

July 31. The federal government threatens striking transportation workers to return to work, or face induction into the army. Buses resume operation as troops move into the city. Strike leaders are arrested for violation of the Smith-Connally Act.

August 1. Riots by operators of the Philadelphia Transportation Company erupt when light black workers are upgraded in their employment. Workers jeer the plea of army and navy officers to return to their jobs so that they may aid the war effort.

August 3. Roosevelt orders the army to take over the transportation system when TWU members refuse to end their strike. The War Department expresses fears that critical war materials are being blocked.

August 4. The army asks the city police to aid its efforts when strikers defy their attempt to run the railroads.

August 6. Striking workers return to their jobs, and service is resumed on public transportation.

August 9. Black trainees return to their jobs.

August 17. Federal troops are removed from the city, and the public transportation system is returned to company management.

1945      May 24. The Pennsylvania legislature passes the Pennsylvania Urban Redevelopment Law, aimed at rehabilitating the slums of Phildelphia.

August 6. New Jersey residents, working at the Philadelphia Navy Yard, strike against the city wage tax, but return to work two days later.

September. The city creates the Redevelopment Authority to work for the reconstruction of the slums.

November 24. City employees request a wage hike.

1946      May 5. A special squad to combat black markets in scarce goods is organized within the police department.

June.     Bonds are issued to finance the purchase of voting machines and other local improvements.

November 20. The city plans coal conservation in case miners decide to strike.

1947      September 6. The Better Philadelphia Exhibition opens.

November.     Mayor Samuel defeats the bid of R. Dilworth, a Democrat, in the mayoralty contest.

December 28. The All-Negro Police Squad is praised for its record.

1948          June. Both the Republicans and Democrats hold their na-
              tional conventions in Philadelphia.

1949          January 6. The city council approves a pact with the state
              to redevelop the area around Independence Hall.

              April 28. Fire Marshall G.J. Gallagher is convicted for
              extortion, bribery, and conspiracy.

              August. Gallagher is impeached from his position as Fire
              Marshall.

              December 3. The city council plans to raise income taxes
              in an effort to balance the budget. The decision is opposed
              by both business and labor.

1950          September 27. A grand jury indicts plumbing inspectors
              and union officials on charges of extortion.

1951          April 17. Voters approve a new home rule municipal char-
              ter. The Taxes Receiver is replaced by a seventeen-man
              council and an appointed Revenue Commissioner.

              October 29. Municipal employees win a five-day work week.

              November 7. The Democratic nominee, J.S. Clark, beats
              Dr. Poling, the Republican candidate, in the contest for ma-
              yor. This marks the first Democratic victory in sixty-seven
              years.

              December. A new U.S. Steel plant brings an industrial
              boom to the metropolitan area.

1953          January 29. Plans are announced for a multi-million dollar
              business and shopping development on the site of the Broad
              Street Railroad Station and "Chinese Wall."

1954          Friends Service Inc. completes an eighty-eight unit coopera-
              tive apartment building in order to promote urban renewal.

              July 22. The City Hall Times, a journal for municipal em-
              ployees, is published.

1955          March 3. V.D. Northrop is appointed city managing direc-
              tor.

July 8. Ground is broken for a $20-million transportation building in the Penn Center.

November 8. The Democratic nominee for mayor, R. Dilworth, beats the Republican candidate Longstreth.

1956      June 16. Business and civic leaders weigh a plan for a ten to twenty year $250-million redevelopment of the entire downtown section.

October 6. A 500-acre tract of the Cherry Hill section of Merchantville, New Jersey, is selected for a fully integrated suburb, as a means of diverting Philadelphia residential growth to an area along Route 38.

December. A full-time lobbyist is named for the city.

1957      March 30. The city gets $87,286,000 from the Federal Urban Renewal Administration to finance the redevelopment of the Eastwick lowlands area.

October. The city wins federal funds for the redevelopment of the Society Hill section.

1958      May 29. The world's largest apartment building, a thirty story, 3,300 room house, the Penn Towers, is planned as part of Penn Center.

October 25. The Greater Philadelphia Chamber of Commerce reports that the black population rose from 13 percent of the total in 1940 to 23.4 percent in 1958.

1959      Park Town Apartments and Food Distribution Center are completed. The markets of the city are moved from Dock Street to South Philadelphia.

November 3. Dilworth defeats Harold Stassen in his bid for mayor in a landslide victory for the Democrats. It is the worst Republican setback in Philadelphia.

1960      November 30. A record $288,600,000 budget is signed.

1961      January 21. A new regulation is passed requiring policemen to wear name plates.

February 18. The Redevelopment Authority proposes a

clean-up plan of skid row, an area that costs the city $4-million annually.

May. The Philadelphia Maritime Museum is opened to the public.

May. A twenty-one story municipal services building is planned for Penn Center.

May 27. Mayor Dilworth pledges an active campaign to clean up his administration. Five city aids are ousted, including the city treasurer, for alleged fraud and bribery. It is the first time a Democratic administration is involved in scandal.

June 20. A $70-million industrial park near the North Philadelphia Airport is planned by Tishman Realty.

September. A redevelopment project for the Eastwick and Washington Square areas is begun.

October. A redevelopment project is proposed for City Hall West Plaza. It is to be erected on a site opposite Penn Center.

November. The Redevelopment Authority plans a commercial center opposite Penn Center.

1962    February 12. Dilworth resigns as mayor in response to the uncovering of scandal, which rocks his administration. He is replaced by James Tate, the former president of the city council.

December 1. Philadelphia insists on including art work in its renewal project, the only major city to do so.

1963    May 16. Mayor Tate orders University City to halt the demolition of homes in a predominantly black area, following a demonstration at City Hall.

June 6. The city council approves a code prohibiting racial bias in employment, public accommodations, and housing.

June 8. CORE protests police harassment of local black leaders.

June 26. The Board of Education adopts a policy of racial integration of both students and staff.

September 26. The Board of Education agrees to assign all new qualified teachers to predominantly black schools, in order to reduce the number of substitute members of the faculty. The NAACP drops its suit against the Board once this policy is announced.

November 5. Mayor Tate, with the backing of President John F. Kennedy, wins reelection. In spite of charges that he lacks leadership on racial problems, he wins an overwhelming majority in the black sections of the city.

1964   June 6. The Board of Education announces plans to bus 3,000 students from predominantly black neighborhoods to underpopulated schools.

August 28. Blacks riot in North Philadelphia. They throw bottles and rocks at police and loot stores. Four hundred policemen are dispatched to the area to quell the violence.

August 29. Black bands of youths continue to loot stores. Fifteen hundred policemen keep the rioting contained to scattered acts of violence after Mayor Tate imposes a quarantine on the beseiged section. Barrooms and liquor stores are ordered closed by Governor William Scranton. Business losses are estimated at $3-4 million.

August 31.   The police uncover a cache of weapons in a raid of the headquarters of cult leader Shayka Muhammad, an ex-Black Muslim. Local Republicans score Mayor Tate for not taking sterner measures in the riot, but he defends police restraint.

September 4. The Philadelphia and Taxpayers Association sues to bar the busing of 2,900 students.

September 7. Mayor Tate lifts the curfew from North Philadelphia, as quiet is restored to the area.

November 9.   Ex-Black Muslim leader, S. Muhammad Ali Hassem, is tried for inciting the riots in North Philadelphia.

1965   March 13. The police are authorized to use dogs to patrol elevated stations and subways.

May 15. Approximately 300 NAACP pickets demonstrate
to oppose Girard College's all-white adminssion policy.
The Board of Trustees declares it will not integrate under
mob pressure.

May 26. Philadelphia inaugurates the first program in the
nation of allowing the poor to elect 144 poor neighbors to
represent them in the antipoverty program.

August 17. Black gangs break store windows and burn a
car.

December 10. Two thousand police march in front of City
Hall to demand a pay hike.

December 16. The city and state governments join the suit
by black parents against the segregated admission policy
of Girard College.

1966        April 9. Mayor Tate announces a $3.5-million beautifica-
tion program, half of it to be funded by the federal government.

August 2. Blacks riot in South Philadelphia after the police
attempt to break up a street fight.

August 13. Acting Police Commissioner Rizzo orders raids
of four civil rights organizations in a black ghetto of North
Philadelphia. They discover dynamite in the premises of
the SNCC office.

September 2. A federal court rules that Girard College
may not exclude blacks from admission.

October 2. A redevelopment project at Penn's Landing
port is created.

October 8. Over 1,800 people picket Girard College when
the trustees seek to reverse the ruling of a lower federal
court requiring racial integration of the school. Civil
rights organizations like the NAACP, SNCC, and Black Mus-
lims send representatives. Three leaders of the Ku Klux
Klan are arrested outside of the college.

October. The Philadelphia Industrial Development organization and the Philadelphia Chamber of Commerce sponsor

a $125-million, 650-acre industrial park to stem the flight
of industry to the suburbs. The planned park is to be the
largest such enterprise within a major city of the United
States.

October 23. Mayor Tate announces a $500-million down-
town shopping district renewal plan. The project, to be
publicly and privately financed, includes plans for parking
areas, office buildings, and an underground shopping mall.

November 2. A federal court permanently enjoins Girard
College from refusing admission to any orphan boy on the
basis of his race. It orders seven black children to be admitted, if they qualify on other grounds.

December 18. An $80-million stadium complex along the wate
waterfront area is planned.

1967

January 10. Philadelphia tries to end de facto segregation
by offering superior educational programs in deprived areas.
It is hoped that this scheme will attract students to cross
racial boundaries.

March 29. The civilian Police Advisory Board is abolished
by court order in a suit brought by the Fraternal Order of
Police.

April 23. The city council passes a resolution setting up
a sister-city tie with Tel Aviv, Israel.

May 28. The federal government agrees to appropriate
$6-million to help beautify the Delaware Expressway section
through the historic section near Independence Hall.

June 10. A twelve block area in South Philadelphia erupts
in violence following a dispute between a white and black
merchant. The police seal off the area when youths hurl
rocks and bottles.

June 29. President Lyndon B. Johnson tours the scene of the
1964 riot and visits a new federally funded job training center.

July 27. Mayor Tate announces a limited state of emergency
when scattered disorders erupt in black neighborhoods. Special police riot squads are dispatched to contain the violence.

July 29. Mayor Tate reveals a plan to deploy recruiters in jobmobiles in high unemployment areas who will hire men off the street.

August 3. Tate warns of the continuing potential for riots in the city and requests the city council to broaden his powers to prevent disorders. He meets at a luncheon with 250 businessmen, who promise to work for better race relations by providing 1,500 unemployed blacks with jobs.

August 17. The city council passes new emergency legislation to protect lives and property during a riot.

September. Six members of the Revolutionary Action Movement are held in an assassination plot to poison Mayor Tate, Police Commissioner Rizzo, and several policemen during their unsuccessful attempt to stir a riot on July 29th.

October 7. The Southeastern Pennsylvania Development Fund announces its $1.2-million project to convert Germantown into the Regional Technical Park, an industrial complex.

November 7. Tate is reelected mayor in a narrow victory over Republican District Attorney Specter. A strong Catholic and labor turnout significantly contributes to Tate's success.

November 19. Large numbers of blacks rally to oust Police Commissioner Rizzo. They claim the police acted improperly in putting down race riots. The mayor defends Rizzo.

November 22. Mayor Tate forms a committee to probe charges by blacks of police brutality.

1968        March 14. A $200-million apartment-office-hotel complex, Century Twenty-one, is planned as part of the downtown Penn Center redevelopment area.

April 5. Police Commissioner Rizzo, in response to the assassination of Martin Luther King, proclaims a limited state of emergency. He orders the closing of bars and liquor stores and prohibits large public gatherings.

May 11. Business and civic leaders promise $1-million for a project to help the black community become involved in productive enterprises. The Black Coalition is given the task of administering the scheme.

May 20. The United States Supreme Court upholds a lower court ruling requiring Girard College to integrate.

August 24. Dig This, a black newspaper published by a North Philadelphia street gang and promoted by a local civic organization, centers its writing on the quest of blacks to improve themselves and their community.

September 11. The first black boys to attend Girard College enter the institution.

November. The Greater Philadelphia Movement publishes a brochure illustrating the efforts of the business community to further the social and economic advancement of blacks.

November 25. A nonprofit organization of professionals and businessmen, Greenwall Housing Inc., opens a "supermarket" of social services to combat blight in the Spring Garden section.

December 26. The Philadelphia-Baltimore-Washington Stock Exchange threatens to leave the city when a tax package is signed levying a 5-cent-a-share tax on stock transactions.

1969        January. The Philadelphia-Baltimore-Washington Stock Exchange, to avoid paying a new tax on stock transactions, begins to move to a new location in Bala Cynwyd.

February. A common pleas court declares Philadelphia's new tax on stock transactions invalid, and the stock exchange remains in its old home in the city.

June 28. The Black Panther party opens a chapter in the city. It announces its determination to restructure society.

July 12. The District Attorney's Office probes allegations by white merchants in North Philadelphia that CORE extorts "donations" from them for black projects.

August 15. Residents of North Philadelphia bring suit in federal court to prevent the Nixon administration from transferring control of the model cities program from citizens to the municipal government.

September 13. Mayor Tate, commenting on rising crime statistics and teenage gang violence, calls the Quaker City a "city of fear."

October 10. Police Commissioner Rizzo announces the arrest of four members of a militant black group, Brothers United, for plotting to bomb white establishment groups with stolen hand grenades. The police recover fifty-seven army grenades.

November. An economist of the Federal Reserve Board reports that the shift of industry to the suburbs deprives blacks of job opportunities at a time when their population has nearly doubled from 18 percent of the city's residents in 1950 to 32 percent by 1969.

1970

June 10. Mayor Tate places a nine square mile section of the city under a limited state of emergency in response to several evenings of racial conflicts over the use of a playground.

July. Philadelphia loses its bid to be the site of the bicentennial exposition. The Bicentennial Commission recommends a multi-city program, but selects Philadelphia as one of the major centers, and the one for an international exposition. President Nixon backs this decision.

July 18. Philadelphians contest President Nixon's policy on model cities, and the United States Court of Appeals rules that his Secretary of Health, Education and Welfare, George Romney, has violated the act by drastically reducing the role of local residents.

August 3. The National Pollution Control Administration ranks Philadelphia as one of the ten cities in the United States with the worst composite sulphur oxide levels.

August 30. Several policemen are wounded and one killed in a shoot-out in a black area of West Philadelphia. The suspects are believed to be members of a revolutionary black organization. Black militants claim that the shootings were executions. Tate declares a state of emergency in the racially turbulent North and South side sections.

August 31. The police raid the Black Panther party headquarters and arrest fifteen youths after an exchange of gun-

fire. The Panthers claim the raid is an attempt by the police to suppress their constitutional convention that is to be
held in the city.

December. Knight Newspapers Inc. purchases The Inquirer
and Daily News. The papers issue investigative probes of
police brutality.

December 21. The Commonwealth of Pennsylvania files
suit in a United States District Court charging the Police
Department with discrimination against blacks in hiring and
promotion policies. It argues that the percentage of black
applicants has shrunk to 8 percent in 1970 as compared to
30 percent in 1966. Rizzo denies the allegations.

## DOCUMENTS

These readings are designed to help the student view the environ‐
ment of Philadelphia through the eyes of contemporary participants.
While the selections do not present the entire fabric of this society,
they reflect some of the significant problems and achievements that
shaped the development of the Quaker City. The passages, it is hoped,
will put flesh on the bare bones of the chronological survey and allow
the student to gain an awareness of the tensions and vitality that form
a continuing part of the Philadelphia story.

## THE FRAME OF GOVERNMENT
## 1682

The Charter granted by William Penn to the residents of Pennsylvania on April 25, 1682 established a basis of government that was the most liberal in the colonies. Denying himself the broad powers exercised by early proprietors, he set up a two-house legislature, whose members were to be elected by freemen who owned property or paid taxes.

Source: Pennsylvania Charter, State Archives, Harrisburg, Pennsylvania; reproduced on vellum in Columbia University, March, 1925.

TO ALL PEOPLE To whom these presents shall come THEREAS King Charles the Second by his Letters Patents under the Great Seal of England for the Consideracons therein menconed hath been graciously pleased to Give and Grant unto me William Penn (by the name William Penn Esqr Son and heir of Sr William Penn deceased) and to my heirs and Assigns for ever ALL that Tract of Land or Province called Pennsilvania in America with divers Great Powers Preheminencies Royalties Jurisdiccons and Authorities necessary for the Well-being and Government thereof. NOW KNOW YEE That for the Well-being and Government of the said Province and for the Encouragement of all the ffreemen and Planters that may be therein concerned in pursuance of the powers afore mencond I the said William Penn have declared Granted and Confirmed and by these presents for me my heirs and Assigns Do declare grant and Confirm unto all the ffreemen Planters and Adventurers of in and to the said Province These Liberties ffranchises and Properties TO BE HELD Enjoyed and kept by the Freemen Planters and Inhabitants of and in the said Province of Pennsilvania for ever. IMPRIMIS THAT the Government of this Province shall according to the Powers of the Patent consist of the Governour and ffreemen of the said Province in the fform of a Provincial Council and General Assembly by whom all Laws shall be made Officers Chosen and public Affairs Transacted as is hereafter Respectively declared That is to say. 2. THAT the ffremen of the said Province shall on the Twentieth day of the Twelfth Month which shall be in this present year One Thousand Six hundred Eighty and two Meet and assemble in some fit place of which timely notice shall be before hand given by the Governour or his Deputy and then and there shall chuse out of themselvs Seventy Two persons of most note for their Wisdom Vertue and Ability who shall meet on the Tenth day of the ffirst Month next ensuing and always be called and Act as the Provincial Councill of the said Province. 3. THAT at the ffirst Choice of Such Provincial Council one Third part of the said Provincial Council shall be Chosen to serve for Three years then next ensuing One Third part for Two years then next ensuing and One Third part for One year then next following such Eleccon and no longer and that the said Third part shall go out accordingly AND on the Twentieth day of the Twelfth Month as aforesaid yearly for ever afterward the ffreemen of the said Province shall in like manner Meet and Assemble together and then Chase Twenty ffour persons being one Third of the Said Number to serve in Provincial Council for Three years it being intended that one Third of the whole Provincial Council (always consisting and to consist of Seventy two persons as aforesaid) falling off yearly it shall be yearly supplied by such new yearly Eleccons as aforesaid and that no one person shall continue therein longer than Three years And in Case any member shall decease before the Last Eleccon during his time that then at the next Eleccon ensuing his decease another shall be Chosen to Supply his place for the remaining time he was to have served and no longer. 4. THAT after the ffirst Seven years every one of the said Third parts that goeth yearly off shall be uncapable of being Chosen again for one whole year following that so all may be fitted for Government and have Experience of the Care and burthen of it. 5. THAT in the Provincial Council in all Cases and matters of moment as Their agreeing upon Bills to be past into Laws Erecting Courts of Justice Giving Judgment upon Criminals Impeached and Choice of Officers in such manner as is herein after menconed Not lesse than Two Thirds of the whole Provincial Council shall make a Quorum and that the Consent and approbacon of Two Thirds of such Quorum shall be had in all such Cases or matters of Moment. And moreover that in all cases and matters of lesser moment Twenty ffour Members of the said Provincial Council shall make a Quorum The Majority of which ffour and Twenty shall and may always determine on such Cases and Causes of Lesser moment. 6. THAT in this Provincial Council the Governour or his Deputy shall or may always preside and have a treble Voice And the said Provincial Council shall always Continue and sit upon its own Adjournments and Committees. 7. THAT the Governor and Provincial Council shall prepare and propose to the General Assembly hereafter menconed all Bills which they shall at any time think fit to be past into Laws within the said Province which Bills shall be publisht and Affixed to the most noted places in the Inhabited parts thereof Thirty days before the Meeting of the General Assembly in order to the passing of them into Laws or Rejecting of them as the General Assembly shall see meet. 8. THAT the Governour and Provincial Council shall take Care that all Laws Statutes and Ordinances which shall at any time be made within the said Province be duly and diligently Executed. 9. THAT the Governour and Provincial Council shall at all times have the Care of the peace and Safety of the province and that nothing be by any person Attempted to the Subversion of this fframe of Government. 10. THAT the Governour and Provincial Council shall at all times settle and order the Scituacon of all Cities Ports and Market-towns in every Country modelling therein all publick buildings Streets and Market places and shall appoint all necessary roads and high-ways in the province. 11. THAT the Governour and Provincial Council shall at all times have power to inspect the management of the publick Treasury and punish those who shall Convert any part thereof to any other use than what hath been Agreed upon by the Governour Provincial Council and General Assembly. . . .

## LETTER of WILLIAM PENN
### 1683

In a letter written to the Committee of the Free Society in London on June 16, 1683, William Penn expressed his vision for the development of Philadelphia as a planned city based upon a grid-iron, rectangular pattern. So successful was Penn's model that it became the blueprint for the design of countless cities in the United States.

Source: An extract of a letter from William Penn, Proprietor and Governor of Pennsylvania, to the Committee of the Free Society in London, dated at Philadelphia, 16th 6th month, 1683 in The Municipal Law of Philadelphia. A Digest of the Charters, Acts of Assembly, Ordinances, and Judicial Decisions relating thereto, from 1701 to 1887. Compiled by Charles B. McMichael, Philadelphia: J. M. Power Wallace, 1887.

Philadelphia, the expectation of those that are concerned in this Province, is at last laid out to the great content of those here that are any ways interested therein. The situation is a neck of land, and lieth between two navigable rivers, Delaware and Sckuylkill; whereby it hath two fronts on the water, each a mile, and two from river to river. Delaware is a glorious river; but Schuylkill, being a hundred miles boatable above the falls, and its course north-east towards the fountain of Susquehannah, that tends to the heart of the province, and both sides our own, it is like to be a great part of the settlement of this age. I say little of the town itself, because a platform will be shewn you by my agent in which those who are purchasers of me will find their names and interest.

And its advantages and extent are set forth by the Surveyor General, Thomas Holme.

The City of Philadelphia now extends from river to river two miles, and in breadth near a mile, and the Governor, as a further manifestation of his kindness unto the purchasers hath freely given them their respective lots in the city, without defalcation of any of their quantities of purchased lands, and it is now placed and modelled between two rivers upon a neck of land, and that ships may ride in good anchorage in 6 or 8 fathom water in both, close to the city, and the land of the city level, dry and wholesome, such a situation is scarce to be paralleled.

The model of this city appears by a small draft now made, and may hereafter when time permits be augmented; and because there is not room to express the purchasers' names in the draft, I have therefore drawn directions of reference by way of numbers, whereby may be known each man's lot and place in the city. The city is so ordered by the Governor's care and prudence, that it hath a front to each river, one half at Delaware, the other at Schuylkill; . . . .

AN EARLY BOOSTER TRACT
1698

In order to attract Europeans to migrate to Philadelphia, the
Quaker Gabriel Thomas (1661-1714), wrote a glowing description of the numerous advantages that the city of William Penn
offered to prospective settlers in the late seventeenth century.

Source: Gabriel Thomas, An Historical and Geographical Account of
Pennsilvania and of West-New-Jersey, London, 1698.

IT REMAIN'D WITH VERY LITTLE IMPROVEMENT TILL THE YEAR
1681, in which William Penn Esq; had the Country given him by King
Charles the Second, in lieu of Money that was due to (and signal Service
done by) his Father, Sir William Penn, and from him bore the Name of
Pensilvania.

Since that time, the Industrious (nay Indefatigable) Inhabitants have
built a Noble and Beautiful City, and called it Philadelphia, which contains above two thousand Houses, all Inhabited; and most of them Stately,
and of Brick, generally three Stories high, after the Mode in London,
and as many several Families in each.

The Air here is very delicate, pleasant, and wholesom; the Heavens
serene, rarely overcast, bearing mighty resemblance to the better part
of France; after Rain they have commonly a very clear Sky, the Climate
is something Colder in the depth of Winter and Hotter in the height of
Summer; (the cause of which is its being a Main Land or Continent; the
Days also are two Hours longer in the shortest Day in Winter, and shorter
by two Hours in the long Day of Summer) than here in England, which
makes the Fruit so good, and the Earth so fertil . . . .

It is now time to return to the City of Brotherly-Love (for so much
the Greek Word or Name Philadelphia imports) which though at present
so obscure, that neither the Map-Makers, nor Geographers have taken
the least notice of her, tho she far exceeds her Namesake of Lydia,
(having above Two Thousand Noble Houses for her Five Hundred Ordinary)
or Celisia, or Caelesyria; yet in a very short space of time she will, in
all probability, make a fine Figure in the World, and be a most Celebrated Emporeum. Here is lately built a Noble Town-House or Guild-
Hall, also a Handsom Market-House, and a convenient Prison. The
Number of Christians both Old and Young Inhabiting in that Countrey,
are by a Modest Computation, adjudged to amount to above Twenty Thousand.

The Laws of this Countrey, are the same with those in England;
our Constitution being on the same Foot: Many Disputes and Differences
are determined and composed by Arbitration; and all Causes are decided
with great Care and Expedition, being concluded (generally) at furthest
at the Second Court, unless they happen to be very Nice and Difficult

Cases; under Forty Shillings any one Justice of the Peace has Power to Try the Cause. Thieves of all sorts, are oblig'd to restore four fold after they have been Whipt and Imprison'd, according to the Nature of their Crime; and if they be not of Ability to restore four fold, they must be in Servitude till 'tis satisfied. They have Curious Wharfs as also several large and fine Timber-Yards, both at Philadelphia, and New-Castle, especially at the Metropolis, before Robert Turner's Great and Famous House, where are built Ships of considerable Burthen; they Cart their Goods from that Wharf into the City of Phildelphia, under an Arch, over which part of the Street is built, which is called Chesnut-Street-Wharf, besides other Wharfs, as High-Street Wharf, Mulberry Street Wharf, and Vine-Street Wharf, and all those are Common Wharfs; and likewise they are very pleasant Stairs, as Trus and Carpenter-Stairs, besides several others. They are above Thirty Carts belonging to that City, Four or Five Horses to each. There is likewise a very convenient Wharf called Carpenter's Wharf, which hath a fine necessary Crain belonging to it, with suitable Granaries, and Store-Houses. A Ship of Two Hundred Tun may load and unload by the side of it, and there are other Wharfs (with Magazines and Ware-Houses) which front the City all along the River, as also a Curious and Commodious Dock with a Draw-Bridge to it, for the convenient Reception of Vessels; where have been built some Ships of Two or Three Hundred Tuns each: They have very Stately Oaks to build Ships with, some of which are between Fifty and Sixty Foot long, and clear from Knots, being very straight and well Grain'd. In this famous City of Phildelphia there are several Rope-Makers, who have large and curious Rope-Walks especially one Joseph Wilcox. Also Three of Four Spacious Malt-Houses, as many large Brew-Houses, and many handsom Bake-Houses for Publick Use.

In the said City are several good Schools of Learning for Youth, in order to the Attainment of Arts and Sciences, as also Reading, Writing, etc. Here is to be had on any Day in the Week, Tarts, Pies, Cakes, etc. We have also several Cooks-Shops, both Roasting and Boyling, as in the City of London; Bread, Beer, Beef, and Pork, are sold at any time much cheaper than in England (which arises from their Plenty) our Wheat is very white and clear from Tares, making as good and white Bread as any in Europe. Happy Blessings, for which we owe the highest Gratitude to our Plentiful Provider, the great Creator of Heaven and Earth. The Water-Mills far exceed those in England, both for quickness and grinding good Meal, their being great choice of good Timber, and earlier Corn than in the aforesaid Place, they are made by one Peter Deal, a Famous and Ingenious Workman, especially for inventing such like Machines. . . .

What I have deliver'd concerning this Province, is indisputably true, I was an Eye-Witness to it all, for I went in the first Ship that was bound from England for that Countrey, since it received The Name of Pen-silvania, which was in the Year 1681. The Ship's Name was the John and Sarah of London, Henry Smith Commander. I have declin'd giving any Account of several things which I have only heard others speak of, because I did not see them my self, for I never held that way infallible to make Reports from Hear-say. I saw the first Cellar when it was digging for the use of our Governour Will. Penn: . . .

THE FRAME of GOVERNMENT
1701

On October 25, 1701 William Penn granted a charter to the city of Philadelphia, setting up a closed corporation of a mayor, aldermen, and common council. An undemocratic instrument of government, it authorized the mayor, recorder, and aldermen to settle judicial disputes, enact ordinances, and exercise executive power.

Source: Philadelphia Charter, Recorded in the Rolls Office at Philadelphia, in Patent Book A, vol. 2, page 154, 155, this 11th of 9th month, 1701 in Minutes of the Provincial Council of Pennsylvania, From the Organization to the Termination of the Proprietary Government, Published by the State, II, Philadelphia: Jo Severns and Co., 1852.

To all to whom these Presents shall Come, sendeth Greeting:
Know ye that I have nominated, appointed and ordained my trusty and Well beloved friends, Edwd. Shippen, Jno. Guest, Samuel Carpenter, William Clark, Thos. Story, Griffith Owen, Phineas Pemberton, Samuel ffinney, Caleb Pusey and Jno. Blunston, to be my Council of State for the Govrmt of the said Province of Pennsylvania, and Counties Annexed, of whom any four shall be a Quorum, to Consult and assist, with the best of their advice & Council, me or my Lieutenant or Deputy Governour for the time being, in all Publick affairs and matters relating to the said Govrmt, and to the Peace, safty and well being of the People thereof, and in the absence of me and my Lieut. out of the said Province & Territories, or upon my Lieuts Decease or other incapacity, I do by these Presents give and Grant to the said Edward Shippen, Jno. Guest, Samuel Carpenter, Willm. Clark, Thos. Story, Griffith Owen, Phineas Pemberton, Samll. ffinney, Caleb Pusey and John Blunston, or any five of them, to Exercise all and Singular the powers, Jurisdiction and authorities whatsoever, to me & my heirs, by Vertue of the Royal Charter or Letters Patent of King Charles the Second, given and Granted, that are or shall be necessary for the well governing of the said Province and Territories, and for the Administring, Maintaining & Executing of Justice, & providing for the safty and well being of the said People during such absence, they and each of them, the said Edwd. Shippen, Jno. Guest, Samll. Carpenter, William Clark, Thos. Story, Griffith Owen, Phineas Pemberton, Samll. ffinney, Caleb Pusey and Jno. Blunston, to Continue in Place till my further order shall be known: and I do further hereby grant to my Ltt. Govr for the time being, full power and authority, upon the Decease or removal of any of the said Council, to nominate and appoint others to serve in their place & Stead, also to add to the number of Council now appointed, and to appoint a president of ye said Council, when and so often as my said Lieut. shall see Cause; . . . .

## ARTICLES of the UNION FIRE COMPANY
### 1736

Thanks to the leadership of Benjamin Franklin (1706-1790), Philadelphia became a leader in organizing the resources of the community to combat one of the most fearsome urban hazards, that of fire. The Union Fire Company brought residents together on a voluntary basis to contribute their efforts to a collective battle against conflagrations.

Source: Articles of the Union Fire Company, M.S. Minute Book, Union Fire Company; Library Company of Philadelphia.

(December 7, 1736) We whose names are hereunto subscribed, reposing special confidence in each other's friendship, do, for the better preserving our goods and effects from fire, mutually agree in the manner following, that is to say:

1. That we each of us at his own proper charge provide two leathern buckets and four bags of good osnaburg [coarse linen] or wider linen, whereof each bag shall contain four yards at least and shall have a running cord near the mouth. Which said buckets and bags shall be marked with the initial letters of our respective names and company thus: A.B. & Company; and shall be applied to no other use than for preserving our goods and effects in case of fire, as aforesaid.

2. That if any one of us shall fail to provide and keep his buckets and bags as aforesaid he shall forfeit and pay unto the clerk for the time being, for the use of the company, the sum of five shillings for every bucket and bag wanting.

3. That if any of the buckets or bags aforesaid shall be lost or damaged at any fire aforesaid, the same shall be supplied and repaired at the charge of the whole company.

4. That we will all of us upon hearing of fire breaking out at or near any of our dwelling houses, immediately repair to the same with all our buckets and bags, and there employ our best endeavors to preserve the goods and effects of such of us as shall be in danger, by packing the same into our bags. And if more than one of us shall be in danger at the same time, we will divide ourselves as near as may be to be equally helpful. And to prevent suspicious persons from coming into or carrying away any goods out of any such house, two of our number shall constantly attend at the doors until all the goods and effects that can be saved shall be secured in our bags and carried to some safe place, to be appointed by such of our company as shall be present, where one or more of us shall attend them till they can be conveniently delivered to or secured for the owner. . . .

## A PLAN FOR THE DEFENSE OF THE CITY
### 1747

Benjamin Franklin, outraged by the refusal of
the Quaker-dominated assembly of Pennsylvania
to provide for the defense of the colony during
a time of war, published in 1747 Plain Truth; or
Serious Considerations on the Present State of
the City of Philadelphia and Province of Pennsylvania. In this pamphlet he attempted to rally the
people of the province to subscribe voluntarily
to measures which would secure them from the
attacks of the French, Spanish, and Indian tribes.
By 1755 his efforts were crowned with success,
and control of the assemby passed to other Christian sects.

Source: The Complete Works of Benjamin Franklin, Compiled and Edited
by John Bigelow, Volume II, New York and London: G.P. Putnam's Sons,
1887.

Should the city be taken, all will be lost to the conquered. Therefore,
if you desire to preserve your buildings, houses, and country-seats, your
statues, paintings, and all your other possessions, which you so highly es-
teem; if you wish to continue in the enjoyment of them, or to have leisure
for any future pleasures, I beseech you by the immortal Gods, rouse at last,
awake from your lethargy, and save the commonwealth. It is not the trifling concern of injuries from your allies that demands your attention; your
liberties, lives, and fortunes, with every thing that is interesting and dear
to you, are in the most imminent danger. Can you doubt of or delay what
you ought to do, now, when the enemy's swords are unsheathed, and descend-
ing on your heads? The affair is shocking and horrid! Yet, perhaps, you
are not afraid. Yes, you are terrified to the highest degree. But through
indolence and supineness of soul, gazing at each other, to see who shall
first rise to your succor; and a presumptuous dependence on the immortal
Gods, who indeed have preserved this republic in many dangerous seasons;
you delay and neglect every thing necessary for your preservation. Be not
deceived; Divine assistance and protection are not to be obtained by timorous prayers and womanish supplications. To succeed, you must join salu-
tary counsels, vigilance, and courageous actions. If you sink into effemi-
nacy and cowardice; if you desert the tender and helpless, by Providence
committed to your charge, never presume to implore the Gods; it will pro-
voke them, and raise their indignation against you. . . .
There is no British colony, excepting this, but has made some kind of

provision for its defence; many of them have therefore never been attempted by an enemy; and others that were attacked have generally defended themselves with success. The length and difficulty of our bay and river have been thought so effectual a security to us, that hitherto no means have been entered into that might discourage an attempt upon us or prevent its succeeding.

But whatever security this might have been while both country and city were poor, and the advantage to be expected scarce worth the hazard of an attempt, it is now doubted whether we can any longer safely depend upon it. Our wealth, of late years much increased, is one strong temptation, our defenceless state another, to induce an enemy to attack us; while the acquaintance they have lately gained with our bay and river, by means of the prisoners and flags of truce they have had among us, by spies which they almost everywhere maintain, and perhaps from traitors among ourselves; with the facility of getting pilots to conduct them; and the known absence of ships of war during the greatest part of the year from both Virginia and New York ever since the war began, render the appearance of success to the enemy far more promising, and therefore highly increase our danger.

Perhaps some in the city, towns, and plantations near the river may say to themselves: "An Indian war on the frontiers will not affect us; the enemy will never come near our habitations; let those concerned take care of themselves." And others who live in the country, when they are told of the danger the city is in from attempts by sea, may say: "What is that to us? The enemy will be satisfied with the plunder of the town, and never think it worth his while to visit our plantations; let the town take care of itself." These are not mere suppositions, for I have heard some talk in this strange manner. But are these the sentiments of true Pennsylvanians, of fellow-countrymen, or even of men that have common-sense or goodness? Is not the whole province one body, united by living under the same laws and enjoying the same privileges? Are not the people of city and country connected as relations, both by blood and marriage, and in friendships equally dear? Are they not likewise united in interest, and mutually useful and necessary to each other? When the feet are wounded, shall the head say: "It is not I; I will not trouble myself to contrive relief!" Or if the head is in danger, shall the hands say: "We are not affected, and therefore will lend no assistance!" No. For so would the body be easily destroyed; but when all parts join their endeavours for its security, it is often preserved. And such should be the union between the country and the town; and such their mutual endeavours for the safety of the whole. When New England, a distant colony, involved itself in a grevious debt to reduce Cape Breton, we freely gave four thousand pounds for _her_ relief. And at another time, remembering that Great Britain, still more distant, groaned under heavy taxes in supporting the war, we threw in our mite to her assistance, by a free gift of three thousand pounds; and shall country and town join in helping strangers (as those comparatively are), and yet refuse to assist each other? . . .

# A PLAN FOR EDUCATION
## 1749

Benjamin Franklin, who did so much to make
Philadelphia the leading intellectual center of
the Colonies, saw the need to establish an Academy, which would provide the youths of the city
with a regular education. In his tract, Proposals Relating to the Education of Youth in Pennsylvania, Franklin furnished public-spirited
citizens with utilitarian arguments for supporting such a school. The pamphlet succeeded in
persuading influential men to set up the Academy in Philadelphia, an institution which eventually burgeoned into the University of Pennsylvania.

Source:"Proposals Relating to the Education of Youth in Pennsylvania," 1749
in The Works of Benjamin Franklin, edited by Jared Sparks, Volume I, Boston: Hilliard Gray and Co., 1840.

The good education of youth has been esteemed by wise men in all
ages, as the surest foundation of the happiness both of private families and
of commonwealths. Almost all governments have therefore made it a principal object of their attention, to establish and endow with proper revenues
such seminaries of learning, as might supply the succeeding age with men
qualified to serve the public with honor to themselves and to their country.
Many of the first settlers of these provinces were men who had received a good education in Europe; and to their wisdom and good management we owe much of our present prosperity. But their hands were full,
and they could not do all things. The present race are not thought to be
generally of equal ability; for, though the American youth are allowed not
to want capacity, yet the best ground, which, unless well tilled and sowed
with profitable seed, produces only ranker weeds.
That we may obtain the advantages arising from an increase of knowledge, and prevent, as much as may be, the mischievous consequences that
would attend a general ignorance among us, the following hints are offered
towards forming a plan for the education of the youth of Pennsylvania, viz.
It is proposed,
That some persons of leisure and public spirit apply for a charter,
by which they may be incorporated, with power to erect an Academy for the
education of youth, to govern the same, provide masters, make rules, receive donations, purchase lands, and to add to their number, from time to
time, such other persons as they shall judge suitable. . . .

A PHILADELPHIAN'S REACTION TO THE
BRITISH OCCUPATION OF THE CITY
1777

The diary of Robert Morton vividly records the
reaction of an upper class Quaker youth to the
British occupation of Philadelphia during the
American Revolution. It mirrors the transfor-
mation of an important segment of the city's
population from royalist sympathies to disillu-
sionment with the British when they personally
witnessed the injustices committed by the English armed forces.

Source: "The Diary of Robert Morton" in the Pennsylvania Magazine of
History and Biography, I, 1877.

September 19, 1777
     O Philada. my native City, thou that hast heretofore been so remark-
able for the preservation of thy Rights, now sufferest those who were Guardians, Protectors, and Defenders of thy Youth, and who contributed their
share in raising thee to thy present state of Grandeur and magnificence with
a rapidity not to be paralleled in the World, to be dragged by a licentious
mob from their near and dear connections, and by the hand of lawless power,
banished from their country unheard, perhaps never more to return, for
the sole suspicion of being enemies to that cause in which thou are now engaged; hadst thou given them even the form of a trial, then thou wouldst
have been less blameable, but thou hast denied them that in a manner tyran-
nical and cruel than the Inquisition of Spain. Alas, the day must come when
the Avenger's hand shall make thee suffer for thy guilt, and thy Rulers shall
deplore thy Fate.
     Nov. 22d. -- Seventh day of the week. This morning about 10 o'clock
the British set fire to Fair Hill mansion House, Jon'a Mifflin's and many
others amo'tg to 11 besides out houses, Barns, &c. The reason they assign
for this destruction of their friends' property is on acco. of the Americans
firing from these houses and harassing their Picquets. The generality of
mankind being governed by their interests, it is reasonable to conclude that
men whose property is thus wantonly destroyed under a pretence of depriv-
ing their enemy of a means of annoying y'm on their march, will soon be
converted and become their professed enemies. But what is most astonish-
ing is their burning the furniture in some of those houses that belonged to
friends of government, when it was in their power to burn them at their
leisure. Here is an instance that Gen'l Washington's Army cannot be accused of. There is not one instance to be produced where they have wan-

tonly destroyed and burned their friends' property. But at the last action at Germantown with the same propriety as the British, could have destroyed B. Chew's house, and then would have injured a man who is banished in consequence of his kingly attachment. On the other side they have destroyed most of the houses along the lines, except Wm. Henry's, which remains entire and untouched, while J. Fox's, Dr. Moore's, and several others are hastening to ruin, so that if they want to make any distinction, it is in favor of their open, professed and determined enemies. I went to the top of c. steeple and had a prospect of the fires. A passage being made through the chevaux de frize, several sloops came up to the city this evening. Price of provisions in market on the day of the fleet's coming to the city, Beef --, Pork --, Veal --, Butter --.

Nov. 23d. -- Several reports concerning Lord Cornwallis' expedition, but not to be depended upon. The kitchen at Evergreen burnt by the carelessness of some Hessian soldiers that were in it. The numbers of people who have by permission of Washington been going to Pennapack for these some weeks past for flour at 40 sh. per cwt., c.m., are now stopped by his order.

Nov. 24th.-- Twenty or thirty sail of vessels came up this morning from the fleet that the city now begins to receive. People in expectation that Germantown will be shortly burnt.

Nov. 25th. -- The fleet daily arriving in great numbers. Burnt about one-half of a house near Gloucester belonging to one Hogg, a person that is reported to be an American Patriot. Lord Cornwallis, with the detachm't under his command, arrived in town this ev'g and brought over 400 head of cattle from the Jerseys.

Nov. 26th. -- This morning I had an opportunity of seeing 63 sail of vessels coming to the city between this and the Point. Lord Howe arrived in town this morning. It is supposed that none of the larger vessels will come up to the city. From all appearances I am of opinion that the Army will not follow Gen'l Washington this winter. A report that additional number of soldiers are to be quartered on the inhabitants this winter. Rob't Ritchie of this city, merch't, is apprehended and secured on suspicion of giving intelligence to Gen'l Washington's Army.

## A HESSIAN'S IMPRESSIONS OF PHILADELPHIA
### 1778

> This letter by a German officer in the Hessian
> Jäger Corps, Captain John Heinrichs, expresses
> the disgust of a stranger in Philadelphia with the
> unhealthy physical environment of the city in the
> last quarter of the eighteenth century. Captain
> Heinrichs was stationed during the War of Inde-
> pendence in the southern area of the Quaker City.

Source: The Correspondence of Professor Schlözer of Göttingen, Vol. III,
p. 149. Translated by Miss Helen Bell in Pennsylvania Magazine of History
and Biography, I, 1877.

At Philadelphia on the Neck, Jan. 18, 1778

I received on November 4, your short letter of the 25th of May, directed to "Lieut. H--- in New York, or to Captain H--- at Philadelphia."

My present opinions of America differ very much from those which I
expressed in my former letters. It is true that I could not now picture to
myself an earthly paradise without thinking of a great part of the Jerseys
and Long Island, but not of Pennsylvania! If the Honorable Count Penn should
surrender to me the whole country for my patent, on condition that I should
live here during my life, I would scarcely accept it. And this is the promised land, the land flowing with milk and honey, which so many before us
have praised! You know already that as every North American province has
an especial existence, and is governed according to its own principles, it
must therefore be judged as differently. The packet boat goes to-morrow,
and with it these few and hasty observations on the country and climate.

Among 100 persons, not merely in Philadelphia, but also throughout
the whole neighborhood, not one has a healthy color, the cause of which is
the unhealthy air and the bad water. Assuredly this is not a consequence of
the latitude, for Pennsylvania lies in one of the healthiest degrees, but the
woods, morasses, and mountains, which partly confine the air, and partly
poison it, make the country unhealthy. Nothing is more common here than
a fever once a year, then eruptions, the itch, etc. Nowhere have I seen so
many mad people as here. Only yesterday, as I was dining with a Gentleman,
a third person came into the room, and he whispered in my ear: Take care,
this gentleman is a madman. Frequently the people are cured, but almost
all have a quiet madness, a derangement of mind which proceeds from slug-
gish, not active blood. One cause, perhaps, is that no food here has as
much nourishment as with us. The milk is not half so rich, the bread gives
little nourishment. There is a noticeable difference in the quality of the produce which is brought to market in Philadelphia, from the Jerseys and from
Pennsylvania. . . .

## A CLERGYMAN PRAISES PHILADELPHIA
### 1792

Contemporaries often noted with delight the
amiable physical ambiance of Philadelphia.
Planned by Penn as a community with civic
amenities and geometric regularity, it had
become by the late eighteenth century the
model city of the nation. An Anglican clergyman in the Quaker City, Jacob Duché, sent
letters to England praising the public-spirited,
rational style of life that he encountered.

Source: Jacob Duché, Caspipinas' Letters; Containing Observations on a
Variety of Subjects, Literary, Moral and Religious. Written by a Gentleman Who Resided Some Time in Philadelphia, Dublin: 1792.

Dean Prideaux, in his connection of the Old and New Testament,
speaks of WILLIAM PENN's having laid out his new city after the plan of
BABYLON. Perhaps it might be difficult at this time of day to ascertain,
what this plan was. Be this as it may, I am not so well versed in antiquity
as to be able to pronounce, whether there is the least resemblance or not
betwixt BABYLON and PHILADELPHIA. Of this, however, your Lordship
may be certain, that no city could be laid out with more beauty and regularity than PHILADELPHIA. Its streets cross each other at right angles: those
which run from north to south being parallel to each other, as well as those
from east to west. Notwithstanding the vast progress that has been already
made, a considerable time must elapse before the whole plan is executed.
The buildings from north to south, along the bank of the Delaware, including the suburbs, now extend near two miles, and those from east to west,
about half a mile from the river. But according to the original plan, they
are to extend as far, nay father, I believe, than the beautiful river, Schuylkill, which runs about two miles west of Delaware.
    The principal street, which is an hundred feet wide, would have a no-
ble appearance, were it not for an ill-contrived court-house, and a long
range of shambles, which they have stuck in the very middle of it. This
may, indeed, be very convenient for the inhabitants, and on their market-
days exhibits such a scene of plenty, as is scarcely to be equalled by any
single market in Europe. -- But I am apt to think, that moveable stalls, con-
trived so as to afford shelter from the weather, would have answered the
purpose full as well, and then the avenue might have been left entirely open.
-- The streets are all well paved in the middle for carriages, and there is
a foot-path of hard bricks on each side next the houses. -- The houses in
general are plain, but not elegant, for the most part built upon the same

plan, a few excepted, which are finished with some taste, and neatly decorated within. -- The streets are well lighted by lamps, placed at proper distances, and watchmen and scavengers are constantly employed for security and cleanliness.

Almost every sect in Christendom have here found a happy asylum; and such is the Catholic spirit that prevails, that I am told, they have frequently and cheerfully assisted each other in erecting their several places of worship. -- These places too generally partake of the plainness and neatness of their dwelling-houses, being seldom enriched by any costly ornaments. Here are three churches that use the liturgy and ceremonies of our Church of England; but only two of them are under any episcopal jurisdiction. CHRIST-CHURCH has by far the most venerable appearance of any building in this city; and the whole architecture, including an elegant steeple, (which is furnished with a complete ring of bells) would not disgrace one of the finest streets in Westminster. The eastern front is particularly well designed and executed; but its beauty is in a great measure lost, by its being set too near the street, instead of being placed, as it ought to have been, forty or fifty feet back.

The STATE-HOUSE, as it is called, is a large plain building, two stories high -- The lower story is divided into two large rooms, in one of which the Provincial Assembly meet, and in the other the Supreme Court of Judicature is held -- The upper story consists of a long gallery which is generally used for public entertainments, and two rooms adjoining it, one of which is appropriated for the Governor and his Council; the other, I believe, is yet unoccupied. In one of the wings, which join the main building, by means of a brick arcade, is deposited a valuable collection of books, belonging to a number of the citizens, who are incorporated by the name of THE LIBRARY COMPANY OF PHILADELPHIA. To this library I have free access by favour of my friend and merchant, who is one of the company. You would be astonished, my Lord, at the general taste for books, which prevails among all orders and ranks of people in this city. -- The librarian assured me, that for one person of distinction and fortune, there were twenty tradesmen that frequented this library.

The internal police of this city is extremely well regulated. You seldom hear of any such mobs or riots, as, I am told, are frequent among their northern neighbours. The poor are amply provided for, and lodged and boarded in a very large and commodious building, to which they have given the name of THE HOUSE OF EMPLOYMENT; because all such as are able to work are here employed in the different trades or manufactures to which they were brought up. This building likewise stands upon one of the city squares, and when compleated, will form a quadrangle, as large, and of much the same appearance, as some of our colleges. In passing through the apartments, I observed and pointed out to one of the managers who was so obliging as to accompany me, an inconvenience, which he assured me, would be rectified, as soon as their funds would admit of it, viz. The want of a few little private rooms, for the better accomodation of such poor, as have formerly lived in good circumstances, and whose misery must needs be considerably heightened by their being obliged to board and lodge in the same common and open apartment, with the vilest of their species.

For the sick and lunatic an HOSPITAL has been erected, by private contributions, under the particular countenance and encouragement of the Legislature. -- The building is still unfinished. -- I walked round it. -- but the chief part of his business, had received his education wholly at this school.

The situation of Philadelphia, in the very centre of the British colonies, the manners of its inhabitants, the benevolent and catholic plan of this Seminary, which exceeds any thing I ever met with at home or abroad, together with the moderate expense of a learned education here, are circumstances, which, I am persuaded, must give this College the preference to any that are or may be erected in North-America; and I doubt not but that the inhabitants of the West-India Islands, many of whom have been well-educated, and have an high taste for literature, did they once make the experiment, would soon be induced by the success to prefer an American to an English education, at least for the earlier season of their children's lives. For my part, I must confess, in spite of all my prejudices in favour of our beloved Oxford, that, had I a son, I should certainly choose to let him go through a course of education at Philadelphia College, before I ventured to send him to that University. -- For your Lordship well knows, that what we principally expect from spending a few years at Oxford or Cambridge, are, the opportunities we have there of conversing with men of genius, and forming such useful and agreeable connections, as may contribute not a little to our future happiness in life.

## REACTION TO THE YELLOW FEVER SCOURGE
## 1793

One of the serious hazards of life in Philadelphia
was the seasonal outbreak of yellow fever epidemics. During the summer of 1793 almost 5,000
people perished from the disease. In this selection one of the city's distinguished civic leaders,
Samuel Breck, vividly recollects the devastation
wrought by the scourge when he was a young man
in the city. He recalls the impotence of the municipality in providing effective public health service for its people.

Source: H.E. Scudder, ed., Recollections of Samuel Breck, Philadelphia:
1877.

I had scarcely become settled in Philadelphia when in July, 1793, the
yellow fever broke out, and, spreading rapidly in August, obliged all the
citizens who could remove to seek safety in the country. My father took
his family to Bristol on the Delaware, and in the last of August I followed
him. Having engaged in commerce, and having a ship at the wharf loading
for Liverpool, I was compelled to return to the city on the 8th of September,
and spend the 9th there. My business took me down to the Swedes' church
and up Front street to Walnut street wharf, where I had my countinghouse.
Everything looked gloomy, and forty-five deaths were reported for the 9th.
In the afternoon, when I was about returning to the country, I passed by the
lodgings of the Vicomte de Noailles, who had fled from the Revolutionists
of France. He was standing at the door, and calling to me, asked me what
I was doing in town. "Fly," said he, "as soon as you can, for pestilence
is all around us." And yet it was nothing then to what it became three or
four weeks later, when from the first to the twelfth of October one thousand
persons died. On the twelfth a smart frost came and checked its ravages.
     The horrors of this memorable affliction were extensive and heart-
rending. Nor were they softened by professional skill. The disorder was
in a great measure a stranger to our climate, and was awkwardly treated.
Its rapid march, being from ten victims a day in August to one hundred a
day in October, terrified the physicians, and led them into contradictory
modes of treatment. They, as well as the guardians of the city, were taken
by surprise. No hospitals or hospital stores were in readiness to alleviate
the sufferings of the poor. For a long time nothing could be done other than
to furnish coffins for the dead and men to bury them. At length a large house
in the neighborhood was appropriately fitted up for the reception of patients,
and a few preeminent philanthropists volunteered to superintend it. At the

head of them was Stephen Girard, who has since become the richest man in America.

In private families the parents, the children, the domestics lingered and died, frequently without assistance. The wealthy soon fled; the fearless or indifferent remained from choice, the poor from necessity. The inhabitants were reduced thus to one-half their number, yet the malignant action of the disease increased, so that those who were in health one day were buried the next. The burning fever occasioned paroxysms of rage which drove the patient naked from his bed to the street, and in some instances to the river, where he was drowned. Insanity was often the last stage of its horrors. . . .

### A MODEL MUNICIPAL PRISON: THE WALNUT STREET JAIL
### 1796

> Philadelphia in the eighteenth century often as-
> sumed a role of urban leadership, initiating a
> host of municipal improvements, and in the field
> of penal reform, her prisons seemed to contem-
> poraries to offer a model of humane, construc-
> tive treatment of criminal offenders. Robert J.
> Turnbull in the pages of the Charleston Daily
> Gazette lauded the system of justice he had dis-
> covered in an excursion to the Walnut Street Jail.

Source:  Robert J. Turnbull, A Visit to the Philadelphia Prison; Being An
Accurate and Particular Account of the Wise and Humane Administration
Adopted in Every Part of the Building; Containing Also an Account of the
Gradual Reformation, and Present Improved State, of the Penal Laws of
Pennsylvania: With Observations on the Impolicy and Injustice of Capital
Punishments. In a Letter to a Friend, Philadelphia: Budd and Bartram,
1796.

Premising thus much, and in further compliance with my promise of
writing, I am necessarily induced to give you an account of the Philadelphia
Prison. Notwithstanding a residence in this place for some months, I had
never the curiosity, till the last week, to visit the WONDER of the world.
The expression is comprehensive but no less just; for, of all the Bridewells
or penitentiary houses I ever read or heard of, I have met with none founded
on similar principles, or which could in any manner boast of an administration, so extensively useful and humane. . . .

You must admire, my friend, the excellency of these arrangements.
You perceive, in the first place, there is no intercourse whatever between
the males and females; they cannot even see each other. None again between convicted and untried criminals; nor between either of them and the
vagrants. This must at all times be a desirable object. Persons who have
not been convicted of the charges they stand imprisoned for, ought not, in
justice, to have a connection with, and be placed among, such prisoners as
have been condemned. The difference of their situation demands separation.
On the other hand, as the intention of the new system of laws is not only to
punish offenders, but to restore them reformed to society, it is more absolutely necessary, that the convicts should be kept apart from the vagrants.

It is well known, that in no one place are offered more injurious and
vicious examples, than in a prison, where condemned, untried and all other
classes of prisoners, are intermingled, without regard either to age, sex,
or condition. Those in many parts of Europe, and several in America,

have long stood melancholy evidences of this fact. Thousands are committed annually for a trifling fault or misdemeanor -- many from misfortune
or accident -- and we may venture to assert, that scarcely one has been
dismissed, with the same stock of morality he carried in with him. Accus-
tomed to idleness, debauchery, and practice of frauds upon their keepers,
upon visitors and each other, the young and unexperienced criminal is early
taught to imitate the dexterity of his elders -- the timorous soon acquires
the audacity of his more hardened companions -- the modest become spec-
tators of, and inured to the indelicacy and indecency of others -- and thus,
amidst such frequent opportunities for vice, are planned, not a trifling proportion of the murders, robberies, and other kinds of villany, perpetrated
after their escape or discharge.

In Philadelphia, the separation of the different classes of prisoners
was early deemed an object of the highest importance, by all who were in
any wise interested in the then contemplated reform of the prison government, and as such steadily adhered to. The inhabitants of the prison were
extremely averse to the measure, and were always more emboldened in
their confidence of its failing, from the countenance of their jailer and keepers, who naturally preferred the old system, as it would furnish them with
a greater harvest of perquisites and exactions. Finding at length that the
perseverance of "the society for alleviating the miseries of prisons," bid
fair to an extinction of all hopes of their continuing in the same scene of
confusion, with one consent they resolved on a breach of prison. The attempt was accordingly made on the evening of the day the new order of things
had taken place. Fortunately few of them escaped. The jailer was immediately discharged, and since that period almost every project for the same
purpose has failed, either from the want ot unanimity of the most evil disposed, the fears of those less so, or the decided disapprobation of the greatest proportion of the prisoners, to any thing of the kind.

Nothing appears more grievous to a person long initiated into habits
of indolence and licentiousness, than the idea of being compelled to alter
them. This I hold as an undoubted position; and therefore the constant and
hard labour, to which a criminal is sentenced in Pennsylvania, must be productive (and it has been) of the most beneficial effects. Although humane,
it is a punishment, sufficiently dreadful and severe to excite terror into the
minds of the depraved; and, besides affording an example of true justice,
it is of all others the best adapted for the amendment of the convict himself.
Another thing; as the design of penalties is not only to prevent the commission of crimes, and reform offenders, but likewise to make reparation for
the injury done to society, or one of its members; the last of these objects,
cannot be better obtained, than by the personal industry of the criminal,
while under condemnation. Of this the legislature were no doubt fully persuaded, when they fell upon the present improvement, in matters of juris-
prudence. . . .

## DESIGNS FOR ECONOMIC CONTROL OF THE HINTERLAND
## 1806

Businessmen realized quite soon that urban
growth and leadership hinged on bringing the
hinterland within the economic orbit of their
city. Seeing other urban centers as potential
rivals, who might capture their rural markets,
entrepreneurs attempted to alert their fellow
citizens to the importance of building transportation connections with the West. In the following selection Lewis Tarascon of Shippingport
urged the people of Philadelphia to construct
roads and canals to Western Pennsylvania, if
they did not want to lose this valuable commerce
to New Orleans. Yet, ironically, the measures
he recommended soon proved to be inadequate.
For before long, another competitor, Baltimore,
adopted a new form of technology, the railroad,
that was to wrest much of the trade with the West
from the city of Penn.

Source:  An Address to the Citizens of Philadelphia, of the Great Advantages
which Arise from the Trade of the Western Country to the State of Pennsylvania at Large, and to the City of Philadelphia in Particular. On the Dan-
gers of Losing Those Advantages and on the Means of Saving Them. By
Messrs. Tarascon Junr., James Berthoud and Co., Philadelphia: Printed
for the Addressers, 1806.

GENTLEMEN,

You know the great advantage which the State of Pennsylvania in general, and the City of Philadelphia in particular, derive from their commercial intercourse with the western country. Whoever will take the trouble
merely to look round him and reflect a little upon the subject, will perceive
that, that advantage is not only already immense, but that it is susceptible
of a considerable increase.

Philadelphia at present supplies the western country with a vast quantity of foreign merchandise, and the State at large furnishes it with a variety
of articles of its own manufacture. The western country on the other hand,
supplies Pennsylvania with Hemp, Cotton, Flax, Bees-Wax, Ginseng, Peltries, Salt-petre, &c. and pays her a considerable balance in cash.

In addition to this, Pennsylvania earns a considerable sum of money
by the carriage backwards and forwards of all that merchandize, which is

continually, by means of an immense number of waggons, traversing its whole whole length between Pittsburgh and Philadelphia, and of the profit of that carrying trade (which at the rate of five and an half cents per pound weight outwards, that is to say) from Philadelphia to Pittsburgh, and of two and an half cents homewards, may fairly be estimated at $250 per waggon, for each journey out and home; no part ever goes out of Pennsylvania.

These advantages give every where a spring to commerce, agriculture, and manufacturing industry; and the City of Philadelphia, which is the only Port within this State, and is the point in which all her commercial relations center receives the greatest benefit from it; for no circumstance can take place which is favorable to the State of Pennsylvania at large, but turns to the advantage of the City of Philadelphia. That those means of prosperity exist, is beyond all controversy, and if Philadelphia takes the proper measures to preserve them, they will be found to increase in the same proportion with the population and riches of our western settlements, in whatever part thereof that increase of population and prosperity may take place.

It is indeed impossible not to be convinced of this truth if one will only take the trouble to cast his eye on a map of the United States, and consider what are the means of commercial intercourse between them: But while we enjoy those advantages and may continue so to do, if we take those measures which the nature of things obviously points out, we are sure to lose them, on the other hand, if those same measures are not immediately resorted to, for it is certain, that the road which lies between Philadelphia and Pittsburgh, is not the natural channel of commercial intercourse between the western parts of the United States and foreign countries; said way may be used only for rich produces, such as Furs, Peltries, Bees-Wax, &c. for a part of those fit for home consumption, and for the articles to be sent from Pennsylvania to those countries. Their bulky commodities, such as Grain, Flour, Timber, Tobacco, Cotton, &c. (and they are the sole by which our western friends may pay the major part of the articles of foreign growth and manufactures, which they stand in need of) would cost more by carrying expenses up the rivers and through our State, than their proceeds would be at any foreign market, and of course such a way can never be practicable for them. They have no other channel than the going down the rivers, and reaching the seas through the mouth of the Mississippi. The nature of things does not allow a choice in the means, we must forcibly comply with it, or lose our share.

It is true that, that channel has not yet been brought into general use; and that the Ohio and the Mississippi, are as yet navigated but by few traders but this is owning to the following causes.

First, This navigation is as yet new, and like all new things require time to be generally followed.

Second, The western traders have not yet had sufficient time to establish the necessary connections at New-Orleans.

Third, The Merchants of New-Orleans have not yet formed the necessary establishments in the western country.

Fourth, The commerce of New-Orleans is not yet established on a sufficiently solid footing. The Merchants there, do not possess sufficient capitals, real and fictitious to make the necessary advances.

Fifth, That no company has yet been formed, for a regular navigation up and down the Mississippi and lower Ohio.*

Sixth, That the western traders are yet in want of credits which they obtain from the Merchants of Philadelphia, and Baltimore, and still remain attached to those Ports, partly from that necessity, and partly from habit.

But the commerce of New-Orleans, is assuming a regular shape. Capitals are accumulating there, men of enterprize and public spirit, already direct their views towards that Port, and the inhabitants of the western country, are considering the means of improving that internal navigation. Commercial connections are forming by little and little, between the upper country and New-Orleans, and as soon as regular course of navigation, up and down the rifer, shall have given rise to regular exchanges at New-Orleans, that Port being always provided with all the articles that are necessary for the consumption of the western inhabitants, because it can procure them from abroad as well as the other Ports of the United States, all the above detailed impediments will disappear, and then, if Philadelphia has not been before hand, in taking proper measures to preserve her due share of the western trade, it will, with all its advantages, flow entirely down to New-Orleans, as rapidly as the waters which nature seems to have destined to waft it, and Pennsylvania and the City of Philadelphia, will lose it for ever.

Although we cannot possibly, nor ought we to endeavour to prevent New-Orleans from enjoying her share of the benefit of the trade of the Western County: yet it is in our power, and we are bound to take all reasonable means to secure to ourselves, that participation in it which our geographical possition, our population, our capitals, and a variety of other favorable circumstances enable us to command, if we but avail ourselves of the means which we have actually in our power. Those means appear to be the following:

First, To improve the roads, and other means of communication be- Philadelphia, and the head waters of the Ohio at Pittsburgh; and between Philadelphia, and the head waters of all the rivers of this state which empty themselves into the Ohio.

Second, To improve the portage between Presqu'isle, and Le Boeuf.

Third, To provide a sufficient number of waggons, on public or private account, to run regularly, speedily, and economically between Philadelphia and Pittsburgh, and the other head waters as aforesaid.

Fourth, To provide a sufficient number of packets, to ply constantly and regularly, between Pittsburgh and Louisville. . . .

---

* We call Lower Ohio that part of that River which is below the Rapids, Upper Ohio that part which is above.

A DEFENSE OF PUBLIC RELIEF
1830

The influential publicist, Mathew Carey, took
up his pen to defend those dependent on public
relief from charges of laziness. He urged
wealthy Philadelphians to contribute to the phil-
anthropic societies of the city. Recognizing that
poverty was not simply a punishment heaped upon
unworthy sinners, he demonstrated that hard-
working seamstresses, deprived of decent wages,
suffered dreadful privations through no fault of
their own.

Source: Mathew Carey,  Essays on the Public Charities of Philadelphia,
Intended to Vindicate Benevolent Societies from the Charge of Encouraging
Idleness, and To Place in Strong Relief, Before An Enlightened Public, the
Sufferings and Oppression under which the Greater Part of the Female La-
bour, Who Depend on Their Industry for a Support for Themselves and Chil-
dren. Philadelphia: Clark and Raser, 1830.

This pamphlet is now presented to the public for a fifth time, and in
an improved state. The opinions of some of the most estimable members
of society, of the highest order of intellect, and of the purest hearts, induce me to believe, that in pleading the cause of a valuable and industrious
class of females -- in placing their wrongs and sufferings before a humane
and enlightened community, if I have not succeeded to the extent of my
wishes, I have not been wholly unsuccessful; that I have fully satisfied those
who have hearts to feel for human misery, and who have duly weighed the
subject, of the utter fallacy of the heartless, withering slang, which charges
the wretchedness and sufferings of the poor to their improvidence, worth-
lessness, and dissipation; that the shamefully reduced rate of female wages
in general, is the parent of a large portion of that wretchedness and those
sufferings; and that it places those females who depend on their needles,
and live in their own apartments, in a situation almost too trying for human
nature, with five choices -- to beg -- to depend on the overseers of the
poor, a species of begging -- to steal -- to starve -- or to sell themselves
to pollution -- to misery and disease here, and perhaps to misery hereafter.
Scepticism itself can scarcely entertain a shadow of doubt on the subject,
when it is considered that neither skill, talent, nor industry, can enable
those poor creatures to earn more than a dollar, a dollar and a quarter, or
perhaps one out of ten or twenty, a dollar and a half per week, even if fully
employed; that a considerable portion of their time they are unemployed;
that they generally pay half a dollar per week for their lodgings; that they

purchase wood by the small bundle, at the rate, probably, of twelve or fifteen dollars a cord, and all other articles they consume at most exorbitant
prices. These are harrowing truths, which cannot be too often repeated,
until a remedy, or at least some palliation, is applied.

I have, moreover, I hope, established the fallacy of the idea, that benevolent and assistance societies foster idleness and improvidence, by in-
ducing a reliance on their aid, instead of industry and application. This is,
I repeat, in the most earnest manner, a pernicious error, and productive
of masses of misery to the poor, by searing the hearts of the opulent, of
whom many do not require any such plea to induce them to withhold from
the poor that degree of aid and comfort which their boundless means would
enable them to afford, and to which humanity may fairly lay claim. From
the view I have given of the wages of various kinds of female labour, it is
obvious that the aid of those societies, judiciously extended, cannot fail to
be frequently imperiously necessary, and eminently beneficial, and in numerous instances to rescue individuals of delicate and praiseworthy feelings,
from become dependent on the overseers of the poor, and thus a public bur-
den.

It has been confidently, but most erroneously asserted, that the expenditure, in this city, for the support of the poor, as well by individuals
and charitable societies, as by the guardians, is $600,000 a year. This
has excited a spirit of hostility against those societies, among many of our
citizens, and a murmuring at what they regard as an enormous abuse. Few
greater errors have ever had currency. The poor tax, under its worst
management, and nothing could well be worse than it has been prior to the
new arrangement, has generally averaged about $125,000 per annum,
no small portion of which arose from the wretchedness created by the miserable wages paid for female labour. The total receipts of the thirty-three
societies, enumerated in a subsequent page, were, in the year 1828, only
$59,000, of which at least $20,000 consisted of large bequests and donations,
which were invested as capital stock, and of course were unexpended. Thus
the actual expenditure was reduced to less than 40,000 dollars, for all those
societies; for the support of infant schools, and education generally; for the
support of orphan houses; for the widows' asylum, the asylum for the deaf
and dumb, and for the Magdalens; for the house of refuge; for the abolition
of slavery; for colonization; and for purchasing food for the hungry, drink
for the thirsty, and clothes for the naked, exclusive of the government and
county contributions to the house of refuge, and the institution for the deaf
and dumb. I am persuaded that the disbursements of all the other societies,
of every description, benevolent, moral, and religious, would not amount
to half as much more. . . .

I have endeavoured to prove in various parts of this pamphlet, that
the industry, morals, and virtue of the poor, are underrated. A striking
instance of the industry of the female portion of them, is afforded by the
fact, that on Tuesday last, there were elven hundred applicants seeking for
employment at the apartment of the Provident Society, in making shirts at

12 1/2 cents each, although it was known none could have more than four, and few more than two per week, at 12 1/2 cents each. Many of them had travelled six, eight, and ten squares, and some of them from Kensington, a distance of two miles, for this most miserable employment. This bears the most overwhelming testimony to their intense distress, and their untiring industry. . . .

There is one portion of the evils resulting from the present state of things, as regards the rate of wages, paid for most species of female labour, to which no attention is paid, but which is of a most serious character. Those women who have children, and are unable to procure food for them, frequently send them abroad to beg. They are generally repulsed. Hunger pinches them. They have no distinct notions of right or wrong. Their employment degrades and debases them. Temptation arises. An opportunity offers to filch and steal. They avail themselves of it, and it is not improbable that the career of wickedness, which leads so many to the penitentiary, may have commenced in this way, by petty thefts, produced by the goadings of hunger. . . .

In the city and liberties of Philadelphia, there are about 150,000 inhabitants, and, according to the usual proportion, about 25,000 houses. It may be assumed that two-fifths of those houses are occupied by persons in tolerably easy circumstances, who would generally be disposed, on proper application and correct information on the subject, to contribute two or three dollars per annum towards purposes of obvious utility or benevolence, such as the promotion of education, the support of the dispensaries, of the house of refuge, of the establishments for widows and orphans, of the Magdalen asylum, of the asylum for the deaf and dumb, or for the relief of the hungry and naked. To doubt this would be a reflection on the character of the city. If this assumption were realized, it would form an annual fund, of above $20,000, for great objects to which no man, possessed of a spark of grace or goodness, can be indifferent; a fund which would produce immense benefits, and mitigate masses of human misery. . . .

## THE CITY'S GREAT BENEFACTOR: THE WILL OF STEPHEN GIRARD
## 1830

Stephen Girard, the wealthy merchant, was the
great public benefactor of Philadelphia. When he
died, he left almost his entire estate to the city,
earmarking large sums for various municipal
improvements. One of the most enduring monuments of this legacy has been Girard College, a
school originally established to provide poor
white male orphans with an education.

Source: Will of Stephen Girard, Dated February 16, 1830. Proved December 31, 1831. Recorded Philadelphia Will Book, 10, p. 198 in Semi-centen-
nial of Girard College. Biographical Sketch of Stephen Girard. His Will,
and Other Papers Relating to the College and Its Development. Account of
the Exercises on the Occasion of the Celebration of the Opening of the College, January 3, 1898. Edited by George P. Rupp, Philadelphia: Girard
College, 1898.

I, Stephen Girard, of the City of Philadelphia, in the Commonwealth
of Pennsylvania, mariner and merchant, being of sound mind, memory,
and understanding, do make and publish this my last will and testament, in
manner following, that is to say. . . .

I. I give and bequeath unto "The Contributors to the Pennsylvania
Hospital, " of which corporation I am a member, the sum of thirty thousand
dollars, upon the following conditions, namely, that the said sum shall be
added to their capital, and shall remain a part thereof forever, to be placed
at interest and the interest thereof to be applied, in the first place to pay
my black woman Hannah (to whom I hereby give her freedom) the sum of
two hundred dollars per year, in quarterly payments of fifty dollars each
in advance, during all the term of her life; and, in the second place, the
said interest to be applied to the use and accommodation of the sick in the
said hospital, and for providing and at all times having competent matrons,
and a sufficient number of nurses and assistant nurses, in order not only to
promote the purposes of the said hospital, but to encrease this last class of
useful persons much wanted in our city:

II. I give and bequeath to "The Pennsylvania Institution for the Deaf
and Dumb" the sum of twenty thousand dollars, for the use of that institution:

III. I give and bequeath to "the Orphan Asylum of Philadelphia" the
sum of ten thousand dollars for the use of that Institution:

IV. I give and bequeath to "the Comptrollers of the Public schools for
the city and county of Philadelphia" the sum of ten thousand dollars for the
use of the schools upon the Lancaster system, in the first section of the first
school district of Pennsylvania.

V. I give and bequeath to "The Mayor, Aldermen and Citizens of Philadelphia, " the sum of <u>ten</u> <u>thousand</u> <u>dollars</u>, in trust safely to invest the same in some productive fund, and with the interest and dividends arising therefrom to purchase fuel between the months of March and August in every year forever, and in the month of January in every year forever distribute the same, amongst poor white house-keepers and room-keepers, of good character, residing in the city of Philadelphia. . . .

XX. And whereas I have been for a long time impressed with the importance of educating the poor, and of placing them by the early cultivation of their minds and the development of their moral principles, above the many temptations, to which, through poverty and ignorance they are exposed; and I am particularly desirious to provide for such a number of poor male white orphan children, as can be trained in one institution, a better education as well as a more comfortable maintenance than they usually receive from the application of the public funds: And whereas, together with the object just adverted to I have sincerely at heart the welfare of the city of Philadelphia, and, as a part of it, am desirious to improve the neighborhood of the river Delaware, so that the health of the citizens may be promoted and preserved, and that the eastern part of the city may be made to correspond better with the interior: Now, I do give devise and bequeath <u>all</u> <u>the</u> <u>residue</u> <u>and</u> <u>remainder</u> <u>of</u> <u>my</u> <u>real</u> <u>and</u> <u>personal</u> <u>estate</u> of every sort and kind and wheresoever situate (the real estate in Pennsylvania charged as aforesaid) unto "The Mayor, aldermen and citizens of Philadelphia their successors and assigns in trust to and for the several uses intents and purposes hereinafter mentioned and declared of and concerning the same, that is to say: So far as regards my real estate in Pennsylvania, in trust, that no part thereof shall ever be sold or alienated by the said The Mayor Aldermen and citizens of Philadelphia or their successors, but the same shall forever thereafter be let from time to time to good tenants, at yearly or other rents and upon leases in possession not exceeding five years from the commencement thereof, and that the rents issues and profits arising therefrom shall be applied towards keeping that part of the said real estate situate in the city and Liberties of Philadelphia constantly in good repair (parts elsewhere situate to be kept in repair by the tenants thereof respectively) and towards improving the same whenever necessary by erecting new buildings, and that the nett residue (after paying the several annuities herein before provided for) be applied to the same uses and purposes as are herein declared of and concerning the residue of my personal estate: And so far as regards my real estate in Kentucky, now under the care of Messrs Triplett and Burmley, in trust to sell and dispose of the same, whenever it may be expedient to do so, and to apply the proceeds of such sale to the same uses and purposes as are herein declared of and concerning the residue of my personal estate.

XXI. And so far as regards the residue of my personal estate, in trust, as to <u>two</u> <u>millions</u> <u>of</u> <u>dollars</u>, part thereof, to apply and expend so much of that sum as may be necessary -- in erecting as soon as practicably

may be, in the centre of my square of ground between High and Chestnut
streets and Eleventh and Twelfth streets, in the city of Philadelphia (which
square of ground I hereby devote for the purposes hereinafter stated, and
for no other, forever) a permanent College, with suitable out-buildings,
sufficiently spacious for the residence and accommodation of at least three
hundred scholars, and the requisite teachers and other persons necessary
in such an institution as I direct to be established; and in supplying the said
college and out-buildings with decent and suitable furniture, as well as books
and all other things needful to carry into effect my general design.  The said
College shall be constructed with the most durable materials and in the most
permanent manner, avoiding needless ornament, and attending chiefly to the
strength, convenience and neatness of the whole:  It shall be at least one hundred and ten feet east and west, and one hundred and sixty feet north and
south, and shall be built on lines parallel with High and Chestnut streets
and Eleventh and Twelfth streets, provided those lines shall constitute at
their junction right angles:  It shall be three stories in height, each story
at least fifteen feet high in the clear from the floor to the cornice:  it shall
be fire-proof inside and outside, the floors and the roof to be formed of
solid materials, on arches turned on proper centres, so that no wood may
be used, except for doors, windows and shutters. . . .

When the college and appurtenances shall have been constructed, and
supplied with plain and suitable furniture, and books, philosophical and ex-
perimental instruments and apparatus, and all other matters needful to
carry my general design into execution; the income issues and profits of so
much of the said sum of two millions of dollars as shall remain unexpended
shall be applied to maintain the said College according to my directions:

1.  The institution shall be organized as soon as practicable, and, to
accomplish that purpose more effectually, due public notice of the intended
opening of the college shall be given -- so that there may be an opportunity
to make selections of competent instructors, and other agents, and those
who may have the charge of orphans may be aware of the provisions intended
for them:

2.  A competent number of instructors, teachers, assistants and other
necessary agents, shall be selected, and when needful their places from
time to time supplied:  they shall receive adequate compensation for their
services:  but no person shall be employed who shall not be of tried skill
in his or her proper department, of established moral character -- and in
all cases persons shall be chosen on account of their merit, and not through
favor or intrigue.

3.  As many poor white male orphans, between the ages of six and
ten years, as the said income shall be adequate to maintain, shall be introduced into the college as soon as possible; and from time to time as there
may be vacancies, or as increased ability from income may warrant, others
shall be introduced. . . .

## THE SECRET SIN OF THE CITY
## 1845

The lurid writer of Gothic novels, George
Lippard, exposed the secret life of vice that
existed in the seemingly demure and respectable City of Brotherly Love. In his best-sell-
ing shocker, Quaker City, he revealed how
bankers, doctors, lawyers, journalists, and
ministers had created a modern Sodom along
the Schuykill.

Source:  George Lippard, The Quaker City; or, The Monks of Monk Hall.
A Romance of Philadelphia Life, Mystery and Crime, Philadelphia:  Leary,
Stuart and Co., 1876.

### THE LAST DAY OF THE QUAKER CITY

He stood in the wide street of a magnificent city. All around him,
from lofty windows, the glare of many lights flashed out upon the winter
night. Above, the clear cold sky of a calm winter twilight overarched the
far extending perspective, brilliant with light and life, which marked the
extent and grandeur of that wide street of a gorgeous city.

Devil-Bug looked around him, and beheld the sidewalks lined with
throngs of wayfarers, some clad in purple and fine linen, some with rags
fluttering around their wasted forms. Here was the lady in all the glitter
of her plumes, and silks, and diamonds, and by her side the beggar child
stretched forth its thin and skinny arm, asking in feeble tones, for the sake
of God, some charity good lady! And the lady smiled, and uttered some
laughing word to the man of fashion by her side, with his slim waist and ef-
feminate face, she uttered a remark of careless scorn, and passed the
beggar-child unheeded by. Here passing slowly onward, with a look of sanc-
timony, a white cravat and robes of sable, was the lordly Bishop, whose
firm step and salacious eye betokened at once his arrogance and guilt; here
was the man of law with his parchment book and his cold grey eye; here was
the Judge with his visage of solemnity and his pocket-book crammed full with
bribes, and here, hungry and lean, was the mechanic in his tattered garb,
looking to the clear blue sky above, as he asked God's vengeance upon the
world that robbed and starved him.

Devil-Bug rubbed his hands with glee. There was something so exhila-
rating to him, in the sight of all this, in the spectacle of the lofty windows
stored with silks and satins, gold and jewels, enriched with the tribute of
a whole world, in the animation of the sidewalk, its crowds of wayfarers,
its rich and poor, its worldly and its holy men, that old Devil-Bug laughed

gaily to himself and rubbed his hands in very glee.

Wandering slowly onward, he was wrapt in wonder at the magnificence which broke upon his vision, when suddenly a massive edifice rose before him, with long rows of marble columns and a massive dome breaking into the blue of the sky far overhead. Beside this gorgeous structure, which appeared to be in progress of erection, for there was scaffolding about its columns and the implements of the workmen were scattered around; beside this edifice arose a small and unpretending structure of brick, only two stories high, with its plain old-fashioned steeple rising but half-way to the summit of the marble palace. This small and unpretending structure was in ruins, the roof was torn from the steeple, the windows were concealed by rough boards, and from one corner, the bricks had been thrown down.

Devil-Bug, when he beheld this structure in ruins, while the marble palace by its side arose in such grandeur upon the clear blue sky, smiled to himself and clapped his hands boisterously together.

"This," he cried, pointing to the edifice, "this should be the old State House, and I must be in the Quaker City!"

As he spoke, a ghostly form glided from among the gay wayfarers of the sidewalk, and stood by his side, a ghostly form like a thin shape of mist with large dark eyes flashing from its shadowy face. "It is the old State House," whispered the ghostly form, in a voice that thrilled to the heart of the listener. "Yes it is old Independence Hall! The lordlings of the Quaker City have sold their father's bones for gold, they have robbed the widow and plundered the orphan, blasphemed the name of God by their pollution of his faith and church, they have turned the sweat and blood of the poor into bricks and mortar, and now as the last act of their crime, they tear down Independence Hall and raise a royal palace on its ruins!" . . .

"Those chariots are the equipage of a proud and insolent nobility, who lord it over the poor of the Quaker City! Yes, there rides a Duke, and there a Baron, and yonder a Count" This palace is intended for the residence of a king! Liberty long since fled from the Quaker City, in reality has now vanished in its very name. The spirit of the old Republic is dethroned, and they build a royal mansion over the ruins of Independence Hall!". . .

"Cheated the poor out of their earnings, wrung the sweat from the brow of the mechanic and turned it into gold, traded away the bones of their fathers, sold Independence Square for building lots, and built this palace for a King! These are their mighty deeds!". . .

A single voice pealing from among the dead, moving along the street, as they sang the solemn hymn, prayed God to curse the Quaker City.

Then the whole legion of the dead shrieked in one horrible chorus, "Wo unto Sodom! Anathema Marantha!"

"Cursed be the city," cried that solitary voice, leading the supernatural choir. Its foundations are dyed in blood. The curse of the poor man is upon it, and the curse of the orphan. The widow, with her babes starving at her breast, raises her hands and curses it in the sight of God. Wo unto Sodom!" . . .

# A HOUSE OF REFUGE FOR BLACK JUVENILE DELINQUENTS
## 1848

Although a social crusading writer like George Lippard might criticize the Quaker City for its heartlessness, its indifference to the plight of the indigent, Philadelphia nonetheless was taking constructive steps to relieve the distress of the needy. One of the first groups to capture the attention of philanthropists was the street urchin, children who hardly could be accused of being responsible for the degradation of their condition. By mid-century a crusade had begun to save neglected children and reconstruct them from a life of crime. But the City of Brotherly Love, racist in its policies toward the blacks of the metropolis, established a segregated house of refuge for unfortunate black juvenile delinquents.

Source: James J. Barclay, "An Address Delivered at the Laying of the Corner Stone of the House of Refuge for Colored Juvenile Delinquents, on Saturday, July 1, 1848," Philadelphia: T.K. and P.G. Collins, 1848.

The Nineteenth Century will ever be memorable in the history of our country. In it she has risen to rank with the mightiest nations of the earth; her territory has extended from the broad Atlantic to the great Pacific, from the Gulf of Mexico to the Bay of Fundy; her flag floats o'er every sea; her commerce extends to every clime; "her arts, triumphant as her arms are known;" the genius and science of her sons have annihilated time and space, and the most distant parts of our land are united and brought together by her railroads, her canals, and her magnetic telegraphs -- her fields spread forth their abundant harvests, and the skill and industry of her artisans meet with a just reward. In all this, there is abundant cause for congratulation.

But that which sheds the purest luster on a nation, is the interest she manifests in the welfare and happiness of her citizens. A beneficent spirit has pervaded the Union, and on every hand are seen Asylums dedicated to the protection of feeble infancy, and the comfort of declining age -- to the solace of bodily suffering, and restoration of mental sanity. The light of knowledge shines upon the blind, and language has been given to the mute. Amid all these noble charities, one was still wanting, a Refuge for the misguided, the wayward, the erring child. The want of such an asylum was deeply felt, and at the instance of the Philadelphia Society for Alleviating the Miseries of Public Prisons, a general meeting was held in the city of

Philadelphia, on the 4th of February 1826, the Chief Justice of the State, the Hon. William Tilghman presiding, at which it was determined to found a House of Refuge, and measures were adopted to procure an act of incorporation, and to obtain the requisite funds to carry out the plan. The Legislature with great unanimity granted the desired act of incorporation, and the managers zealously, and perseveringly exerted themselves to effect the benevolent object committed to their care. An application was promptly made to their fellow citizens -- the sum contributed was insufficient; another appeal was made -- this did not produce an adequate amount; after a third effort, and the patronage of the State, it was determined to commence the buildings on a limited plan, susceptible, however, of extension, as necessity should require. . . .

The question was frequently asked, "What do you expect to accomplish by the House of Refuge?" The answer was: "We expect to employ the idle, to instruct the ignorant, to reform the depraved, to relieve the wretched, and to enlarge the sphere of virtuous society." And -- "What are the means by which you propose to arrive at the desired end?" "By a firm, kind, and parental discipline; by gaining the confidence and winning the affections of the pupil; by convincing him that his respectability, his usefulness, and happiness are the object of all our endeavors, by impressing on his mind, with constant and zealous care, the important truth, that the path of duty is also the path of happiness; that integrity and industry lead to independence and honor, whilst depravity and idleness bring disgrace, poverty, and punishment; 'that reformation is never hopeless, nor sincere endeavors ever unassisted; that the wanderer may at length return after all his errors; and that he who implores strength and courage from above, shall find danger and difficulty give way before him.' Above all, by using every effort to implant in the youthful heart the principles of piety and religion." Let it always be borne in mind, that a House of Refuge is not a prison; that its object is to save, not to punish. . . .

The House of Refuge is no longer an experiment. More than twenty years have glided away since its establishment. Upwards of 2250 young persons have enjoyed its advantages, and we can now speak from experience. We can see those who were formerly inmates of the Refuge, pursuing a career alike creditable to themselves, and useful to the public -- contributing by their enterprise and industry both to their own honorable advancement, and to the general prosperity. We find the valued and respected citizen, the affectionate husband, the virtuous wife, and the tender parent. . . .

## TURBULENT CLUBS AND TRANQUIL RETREATS OF PHILADELPHIA
### 1848

The sensational writer of urban exposés, George
G. Foster, published a series of articles in the
New York Tribune, which vividly dissected the
various layers of Philadelphia society. The first
selection examines an important social institution,
the fire-house clubs, staffed by ruffian youths,
the so-called b'hoys of the city, who brought dis-
ruption and violence whenever a conflagration
gave them a chance to battle a rival gang of another engine house: the second, describes the
peaceful retreats from urban life available to
Philadelphia dwellers at Laurel Hill Cemetery
and Wissahiccon Creek.

Source: New York Tribune, October 30, 1848 and November 30, 1848.

### SLICE III. THE ROWDY CLUBS

We devote this paper to an effort to rescue the reputation of Philadelphia and Philadelphia Firemen from an odium so general as to appear almost
impossible to be the result of misrepresentation and calumny. And yet such
is the fact. Those who are familiar with the process of making newspapers
know how naturally it is for the unthinking subs of the daily press to indulge
in sneers at the affairs of rival cities, and to distort occurrences for the
purpose of attaching odium to whole classes and communities for the acts
of a few wicked individuals, whose types are abundant in every city. So it
has been with Philadelphia. The Firemen, the authorities, and even the
city itself, have acquired a reputation for rowdyism and brutality, altogether
undeserved, simply from the attrocities [ sic ] of gangs of ruffians and row-
dy apprentices, who do not regularly belong to the Fire Companies at all,
and for the most part are not citizens of Philadelphia. Nine-tenths of those
whose rascalities have made Philadelphia so unjustly notorious live in the
dens and shanties of the suburbs, and are as much detested by the Firemen
as by all other good citizens.

It must be remembered that the City of Philadelphia extends only from
Lombard-street on the South to Vine-street on the North, and from the Delaware to the Schuylkill. Within this space riots and mobs are unknown, and
even disorderly scenes of the mildest character extremely rare. Beyond
the city on the North are the immense suburbs or "districts" of Spring Garden, Northern Liberties, Kensington and Penn Township, and on the South,
Southwark and Moyamensing. Each of these districts has its own separate

municipal organization and elects its own corporation (technically "Commissioners") and all subordinate officers, has its own Police, water, gas, &c, &c., and is entirely independent of the corporate authorities of the City of Philadelphia. These districts were, before the Native American excitements, entirely and immovably Loco-Focoish; and those who know how that party manages and abuses power will readily understand that, in their hands, they have become infested with a set of the most graceless vagabonds and unmitigated ruffians, tolerated by the authorities because their votes were necessary to keep them in office. That most odious and disgusting of all characters, the B'hoy, with which the Stage in New-York and Philadelphia has recently achieved its crowning disgrace, inevitably flourished under this state of things, and has actually a lower and more thorough development of debasement in Philadelphia than in New-York. The districts, especially of Southwark and Moyamensing, swarm with these loafers, who, brave only in gangs, herd together in squads or clubs, ornamented with such outlandish titles as "Killers," "Bouncers," "Rats," "Stingers," "Nighthawks," "Buffers," "Skinners," "Gumballs," "Smashers," "Whelps," "Flayers," and other appropriate and verminous designations, which may be seen in any of the suburbs written in chalk or charcoal on every deadwall, fence and stable-door. These clubs possess a kind of barbarous organization and hold nightly conclaves on the corners of by-streets or in unoccupied building-lots, sneaking about behind the rubbish-heaps, and perhaps now and then venturing out to assault an unprotected female or knock down a lonely passenger. One of their favorite tricks is to raise a false alarm of fire and then make a rush for the engine-houses, pushing aside the regular firemen and assuming their places at the ropes. In this way they gradually usurped control of two or three engines and apparatuses, and and finally drove away the respectable members of the companies, who chose rather to give up their property than to incur the disgrace of such ruffianly association. From these companies, thus transmuted, and strengthened by any number of "outsiders" on either side, have arisen the innumerable fights and atrocities, from the odium of which Philadelphia has so much and so justly suffered. . . .

Slice V. THE WISSAHICCON, THE FALLS, AND LAUREL HILL. Six or seven miles north from Philadelphia on the Wissahiccon Creek, lies the wildest and most utterly undefaced of Nature's quiet haunts. There is nothing in the scene that rises to absolute sublimity crushing the soul with its vast magnificence and forcibly recalling man to a contemplation of his own littleness. But as a type of the fresh, the silent and the picturesque there is perhaps nothing in America to surpass it. Although unlike in its details from Trenton Falls, yet our first visit reminded us at every step of that sacred and spirit-haunted retreat. Yet the Wissahiccon has no dizzy precipices nor yawning chasms, no white-robed cascades leaping madly into foamy abysses. A simple little stream, clambering awkwardly down a primitive dam, above which leans against the hillside an old disabled mill, flows silent and deep as dreamless slumber along a rocky and wall-like bank, thickly covered with trees, and gradually receding to a steep slope on the western side, while the stream expands into a narrow lake, in whose bosom the unmoving images of the trees lose and multiply themselves. The other bank is level for a few rods, and then mounts an abrupt and steep ascent, corresponding to the other face of the ravine. The undergrowth on the eastern bank has been cleared away, leaving nothing but large and noble trees, to the branches of which rude swings have been attached. A primitive low cabin and a long open shed, for the accomodation of visiters and their horses, are the only other signs of civilization which the place affords, if we except half-a-dozen rowboats, the largest covered with an awning, which lie quietly with their noses in the grass, waiting the pressure of pretty feet and the persuasion of the oar, to steal lazily out into the stream.

Such is Wissahiccon, one of the favorite Summer resorts of Philadelphia, and the most soothing, peace-imparting and heart-strengthening retreat into whose blessed shadows "circumstances" have ever had the honor of conducting us. . . .

About three-quarters of a mile this side of the Log Cabin at the Wissahiccon are the Falls of Schuylkill, no great shakes of a cataract, to be sure, but widely celebrated for the "Catfish and Coffee" served there, by Evans and John Nisell. Their taverns, situated on the bank of a dusty macadamized road, offer no very strong external inducements; but they are much frequented for the fresh-caught catfish, coffee and waffles for which they are so well known. To the excellence of the catfish and the plain and savory manner of serving them up we are bound to bear testimony. The waffles, too, are of the genuine old coinage, and they "keep a bringing of 'em, " hot and tempting, until you can no more. The Falls is the great stopping-place for those who visit the Wissahiccon; and not to have had catfish and coffee at Nisell's or Evans's is a positive and unpardonable breach of the etiquette of the road.

In going to the Wissahiccon, or if you prefer it, in returning, you can pass Laurel Hill Cemetery, one of the most exquisitely beautiful gardens of the dead which ever the heart of affection conceived or the hand of taste embellished. In this indescribably lovely spot, whose great and varied natural advantages have been enhanced and absolutely glorified by the genius and love of the living who there make beautiful the resting place of the beloved dead, lies peacefully mingling the dust of the eminent and the humble, the old, the young, the pure, the wise, while over the little mounds which rise like motionless waves of the sea of death, springs a world of flowers, wreathing the white grave-stones and climbing the sculptured monuments, to pour their wealth of perfume upon the air. The narrow apartments of the dead are grouped in family homes, each household enclosed in rich and costly iron railing and furnished with iron chairs, where the living may come and hold communion with their departed kinsfolk, and, half concealed in the exuberant flower-foliage that spreads its rosy tracery all over this solemn yet lovely spot, weep or dream, each according to his mood. . . .

## MUNICIPAL CORRUPTION
### 1848

Increasingly publicists were throwing the spotlight
on the machinations of municipal officials who were
enriching themselves from the administration of
the law. A member of the Philadelphia Bar, using
the pseudonym of Junius, tried to alert the electorate to the corrupt practices that were making a
mockery of the city's system of justice.

Source: The Letters of Junius; Exposing to the Public, For Their Benefit,
the Mal-Practices in the Administration of the Law, the Corruption in the
Offices of the State House Row, in the County of Philadelphia, the Extortions
Practiced by the Public Officers, to which is added, The Legal Fees As
Prescribed by Statutes For Every Public Officer, with Directions to Enable
the Public To Guard Themselves Against the Plunder of the Officers: And
the Mode By Which They May Enforce and Recover the Penalty against Ex-
tortion. Written by An Experienced Member of the Philadelphia Bar, Philadelphia: Printed for the Publisher, 1848.

### POLICY OF STATE -- INSTABILITY OF LEGISLATION --
### ATTACK UPON THE COUNTY TREASURY -- ABUSES IN THE
### CRIMINAL COURT, &c.

In the early history of our Commonwealth, laws were enacted for the
benefit of the people under the democratic policy of "doing the greatest good
to the greatest number;" but the system is now changed; the policy of state
is changed; the legislature is now composed of men, generally speaking,
who go to Harrisburg to serve some particular friends, or to obtain some
special object of pecuniary interest to themselves. There is no longer any
stability in legislation. Laws for the most part are special in their tendency,
and local in their operation. Every man can have an act passed to carry
out his own project. Some to annul trusts -- others to destroy titles --
others to make wills valid of void by law; others to sell real estate; others
to relieve debtors from their obligations, and others to discharge offenders
for trespasses by them committed; others to nullify the decisions of the Supreme Court. In a word, the whole policy of our legislature for the last
ten years has been to legislate the money out of the pockets of one man or
set of men, into the pockets of another. And under this policy, an Act of
the Legislature of Pennsylvania, passed the 22d of April, 1846, pamphlet
laws, page 477, sections 4, 5, and 6, authorizes and directs the Attorney
General, in case of a forfeiture of a recognizance in the Courts of Oyer and
Terminer and General Jail Delivery and Quarter Sessions of the Peace of

Philadelphia, which shall have been entered into before either of the Judges
of said Court or Aldermen of the city, to sue the same out forthwith, and
to prosecute the same to judgment, and to account to the Treasurer of the
County for the same, under the direction of the Court, who are directed,
First, to appropriate and pay the cost of prosecution, the officer for arresting, and the Attorney General for conducting the suit -- Second, to pay
such damage as the person sustained by the commission of the crime by
the defendant -- and Third, the residue to pay into the County Treasury.
This law would seem intended to effect three objects. The first to secure
the appearance of the violator of the law to answer; second, to indemnify
the citizen against injury by reason of such crime; and third, to create a
revenue to the county, by which our taxes would be diminished. These are
the ostensible objects; when in truth and in fact, it was concocted by the
Deputy Attorney General and his friends to serve his personal and pecuniary
interest, as well as that of the Clerk of the Court aforesaid, who receive
the same fees as the Prothonotaries of the several Courts of Common Pleas,
for similar services. It is our purpose to expose to the Legislature, now
in session, the operation of this law upon the community, and ask its immediate repeal. We some time since examined the dockets of the Clerk of
that Court, by the kind permission of that officer, and found, that some
two hundred suits had been instituted within the first year after the passage
of the law, that but two had been prosecuted to judgment, and no execution
had been issued upon either of these at the time of our investigation. That
in ninety of the suits, the Court had directed the county to pay the cost,
amounting to one thousand dollars and upwards, all of which goes into the
pockets of the Attorney General, Clerk, and Sheriff. In sixty the Court respited the recognizance upon the defendant's paying the costs. In thirty-
eight nothing had been done except to issue the writ. And two, all told,
prosecuted to judgment. For this service the Attorney General would be
entitled to $270, being $3 in each suit, from the county, and in the suits
respited, $180, and the balance would go to the Clerk and Sheriff. Thus
$1000 is taken out of the pockets of the tax payer, under the special order
of the Judge who presides for the time being, without any equivalent being
rendered. This is not the only evil connected with the administration of
this law. It offers an inducement to the Deputy Attorney General to oppress
the citizen and wrong the county. . . . .

OPPORTUNITIES FOR ECONOMIC SUCCESS
1869

A magnet that drew many people to Philadelphia
in the period that followed the Civil War was the
burgeoning economic opportunities available in
merchandising and manufacture.  A corps of
publicists hawked to contemporaries dazzling
stories of success and instructed the ambitious
on the methods that had allowed Philadelphia's
men of wealth to create their fortunes.

Source:  I. L. Vansant, The Royal Road to Wealth, An Illustrated History
of the Successful Business Houses of Philadelphia, Philadelphia:  Samuel
Loag, 1869.

There exists no "Philosopher's Stone, " but the ROYAL ROAD TO
WEALTH is open to all.  It is found in a careful study of the Lives of our
Successful men, and nowhere better illustrated than among the Eminently
Successful Business Houses of our own beautiful City of "Brotherly Love. "

Such a history we propose to spread before our readers in the following pages, and shall endeavor so to illuminate their paths that all may read
the finger-boards and count the mile-stones thereon, and will thenceforth
have no occasion to exclaim "on what meat do these our Caesars feed that
they have grown so great."

Every house we illustrate in this work, will be readily recognized as
the Pioneer and Representative of its particular Class; standing prominently
forth the "observed of all observers, " the "bright particular star" in the
brilliant galaxy it so conspicuously adorns.  Most of the prominent members of these Houses are still living, many of them comparatively young,
and all wearing the Crown and wielding the Sceptre with which their own
efforts have invested them, with a commendable meekness for the good of
themselves, their fellows and the great Cause of Human Progress.

The data from which this history was compiled: (the items and incidents in the succeeding pages, ) I have for the most part gotten, either directly or indirectly, from some prominent member of the respective houses
I have chosen as subjects of illustration.  Tracing their onward course we
find success attributable, in every case, to making and vending good wares
at reasonable rates, and keeping even pace with the March of Progress.

These combined with honesty, (not as a policy but a principle, ) sa-
gacity, vigilance and unflagging energy are the land-marks of the great
field through which runs the "ROYAL ROAD TO WEALTH. "  The guide-
boards on the road will be found by consulting the Lives and Histories of
those who have already trodden it.  Fortunately for the world no man how-

ever successful can hold a royalty on his mode of doing business, neither does any one of them halt to "cover his trail" or destroy his pontoons after him.

In conclusion let me say that if a careful consideration of History of the eminently Successful Business Houses we illustrate in this work, shall aid any of my readers in securing the Crown and Sceptre, which lay at the end of the "Royal Road to Wealth," my object will have been attained. . . .

In a brief retrospect of the history of this eminently solid and successful House, in tracing their footsteps as they pursued the "ROYAL ROAD TO WEALTH," certain landmarks stand out in bold prominence, which cannot but be of use to others ambitious to follow in their path. In the first place, we find them starting "from the score" with an avowed determination, a clearly defined object -- supreme excellence of workmanship. There is no "royal road" to this goal. It has to be built over many seemingly insurmountable obstacles. Superior excellence of workmanship may be attained by superior skill of workmen. But where are these workmen in sufficient numbers, in times like these, to be found?

So, in the first place, mechanical devices must take the place of skill; and the question present itself with each new conception of design, not can they find men to do such work, but can they make machinery capable of producing the desired result. So the record of the business shows mind, and money expended without stint, in thus making the machinery to make the machines, in an endless scale of sequences.

Before any machine is made, the tools, the gauges, the unerring guides for the workmen, must be made, so that every subsequent machine shall be like the first one, and all parts interchangeable.

Thus, carefully, and with patient industry, each stepping-stone is laid. All complex machinery, like every complex business, is made up of minor parts. The perfection of the whole machine, or success of the entire business, depends upon the care taken in the construction and arrangement of the minor parts; and here -- "multum in parvo" -- is the secret of success, and fully identifies itself with Franklin's financial axiom, "Take care of the pence, and the pounds will take care of themselves." . . .

## MUNICIPAL REFORM
1885

In response to a growing outcry against municipal corruption, the state legislature in 1885
passed the Bullitt Bill, an act which gave Philadelphia a new charter. This new charter attempted to improve the quality of city government
by expanding the authority of the mayor and by
concentrating many of the executive departments
into a more streamlined system.

Source: The Municipal Laws of Philadelphia. A Digest of the Charters,
Acts of Assembly, Ordinances, and Judicial Decisions relating thereto,
from 1701 to 1887. Compiled by Charles B. McMichael, Philadelphia: J.
M. Power Wallace, 1887.

## AN ACT TO PROVIDE FOR THE BETTER GOVERNMENT OF
CITIES OF THE FIRST CLASS IN THIS COMMONWEALTH

SECTION 1. Be it enacted by the Senate and House of Representatives of the Commonwealth of Pennsylvania, in General Assembly met, and
it is hereby enacted by the authority of the same -- That on and after the
first Monday of April, one thousand eight hundred and eight-seven, in cities
of the first-class in this Commonwealth, the executive power shall be ves-
ted in the Mayor and in the departments authorized by this act.

The Mayor shall be the chief executive officer of the city, and shall
be at least twenty-five years of age, and have been a citizen and inhabitant
of the State five years, and an inhabitant of the city for which he may be
elected Mayor, five years next before his said election, unless absent on
the public business of the United States, and shall reside in said city during
his term of service.

The Mayor shall be chosen by a plurality of the votes cast at the municipal election, and shall hold his office for the next term of four years from
the first Monday of April next ensuing his election, and serve until his suc-
cessor is duly elected and qualified, but shall not be eligible to the office
for the next succeeding term. . . .

It shall be the duty of the Mayor --

I. -- To Cause the ordinances of the city and the laws of the State to
be executed and enforced.

II. -- To communicate to Councils, at least once a year, a statement
of the finances and general condition of the affairs of the city, and also such
information in relation to the same, as either branch of Council may from
time to time require.

III. -- To recommend by message in writing to the Councils all such measures connected with the affairs of the city, and the protection and improvement of its government and finances, as he shall deem expedient.

IV. -- To call special meetings of Councils, or either of them, when required by public necessity.

V. -- To perform such duties as may be prescribed by law or ordinance, and he shall be responsible for the good order and efficient government of the city.

The Mayor shall call together the heads of departments for consultation and advice upon the affairs of the city at least once a month, and at such meetings he may call on the heads of departments for such reports as to the subject-matters under their control and management as he may deem proper, which it shall be their duty to prepare and submit at once to the Mayor. Records shall be kept of such meetings, and rules and regulations shall be adopted thereat for the administration of the affairs of the city departments not inconsistent with any law or ordinance, which regulations shall prescribe a common and systematic method of ascertaining the comparative fitness of applicants for office, position, and promotion, and of selecting, appointing, and promoting those found to be the best fitted, without regard to their political opinions or services.

The Mayor shall be ex-officio a member of all boards herein provided for, except the Board of Building Inspectors, and shall have the right as such to participate in their deliberations and proceedings, and vote, whenever he may deem it advisable so to do.

The Mayor may, by a written order to be transmitted to Select Council giving his reason therefor, remove from office any head of department, director, or other officer appointed by him.

During the recess of Select Council he shall have power to fill all vacancies that may happen in offices, to which he may appoint, subject to the approval of the said Select Council at their next session, and if such appointment shall not be rejected within thirty days after said Select Council shall have convened, the same shall be considered confirmed.

The several heads of departments shall present to the Mayor annually, on or before the first Monday of February, a report of their proceedings during the preceding year, and he shall transmit the same to Councils with any recommendations he may think proper to make.

The Mayor may disapprove of any item or items of any bill making appropriations, and the part or parts of the bill approved, shall be the law, and the item or items disapproved shall be void, unless re-passed according to the rules and limitations prescribed by law for the passage of bills over the Mayor's veto.

The Mayor shall, as often as he may think proper, appoint three competent persons to examine, without notice, the accounts of any city department, trust, officer, or employee, and the money, securities, and property belonging to the city, in the possession or charge of such department, trustees, officer, or employee, and report the result of such investigation. . . .

THE BLACK "GHETTO"
1899

The University of Pennsylvania hired Dr. William
Du Bois in 1896 to investigate the condition of
Philadelphia's black population of approximately
45,000 people. Concentrating his field work
among blacks in the Seventh Ward, he system-
atically visited the homes of residents and examined their social gatherings, churches, schools,
and business organizations. The massive statis-
tical data he gathered enabled him to present a
comprehensive body of facts that eloquently testi-
fied to the brutal environment faced by the black
community.

Source: William E. B. Du Bois, The Philadelphia Negro, A Social Study,
Philadelphia: Publications of the University of Pennsylvania, Series in Political Economy and Law, 1899.

The accommodations furnished for the rent paid must now be considered. The number of rooms occupied is the simplest measurement, but
is not very satisfactory in this case owing to the lodging system which
makes it difficult to say how many rooms a family really occupies. A very
large number of families of two and three rent a single bedroom and these
must be regarded as one-room tenants, and yet this renting of a room often
includes a limited use of a common kitchen; on the other hand this sub-rent-
ing family cannot in justice be counted as belonging to the renting family.
The figures are:

829 families live in 1 room, including families lodging, or 35.2 per cent.
104    "      "    " 2 rooms . . . . . . . . . . . . . or  4.4    "
371    "      "    " 3 "      . . . . . . . . . . . . or 15.7    "
170    "      "    " 4 "
127    "      "    " 5 "      . . . . . . . . . . . . or 12.7    "
754    "      "    " 6 "      or more . . . . . . . . or 32.0    "

The number of families occupying one room is here exaggerated as
before shown by the lodging system; on the other hand the number occupying six rooms and more is also somewhat exaggerated by the fact that not
all sub-rented rooms have been subtracted, although this has been done as
far as possible.

Of the 2441 families only 334 had access to bathrooms and water-
closets, or 13.7 per cent. Even these 334 families have poor accommodations in most instances. Many share the use of one bath-room with one or

more other families. The bath-tubs usually are not supplied with hot water and very often have no water-connection at all. This condition is largely owing to the fact that the Seventh Ward belongs to the older part of Philadelphia, built when vaults in the yards were used exclusively and bathrooms could not be given space in the small houses. This was not so unhealthful before the houses were thick and when there were large back yards. Today, however, the back yards have been filled by tenement houses and the bad sanitary results are shown in the death rate of the ward.

Even the remaining yards are disappearing. Of the 1751 families making returns, 932 had a private yard 12 x 12 feet, or larger; 312 had a private yard smaller than 12 x 12 feet; 507 had either no yard at all or a yard and outhouse in common with the other denizens of the tenement or alley.

Of the latter only sixteen families had water-closets. So that over 20 per cent and possibly 30 per cent of the Negro families of this ward lack some of the very elementary accommodations necessary to health and decency. And this too in spite of the fact that they are paying comparatively high rents. Here too there comes another consideration, and that is the lack of public urinals and water-closets in this ward and, in fact, throughout Philadelphia. The result is that the closets of tenements are used by the public. . . .

This is the origin of numbers of the blind alleys and dark holes which make some parts of the Fifth, Seventh and Eighth Wards notorious. The closets in such cases are sometimes divided into compartments for different tenants, but in many cases not even this is done; and in all cases the alley closet becomes a public resort for pedestrians and loafers. The back tenements thus formed rent usually for from $7 to $9 a month, and sometimes for more. They consist of three rooms one above the other, small, poorly lighted and poorly ventilated. The inhabitants of the alley are at the mercy of its worst tenants; here policy shops abound, prostitutes ply their trade, and criminals hide. Most of these houses have to get their water at a hydrant in the alley, and must store their fuel in the house. These tenement abominations of Philadelphia are perhaps better than the vast tenement houses of New York, but they are bad enough, and cry for reform in housing.

The fairly comfortable working class live in houses of 3-6 rooms, with water in the house, but seldom with a bath. A three room house on a small street rents from $10 up; on Lombard street a 5-8 room house can be rented for from $18 to $30 according to location. The great mass of comfortably situated working people live in houses of 6-10 rooms, and sub-rent a part or take lodgers. A 5-7 room house on South Eighteenth street can be had for $20; on Florida street for $18; such houses have usually a parlor, dining room and kitchen on the first floor and two to four bedrooms, of which one or two are apt to be rented to a waiter or coachman for $4 a month, or to a married couple at $6-10 a month. The more elaborate houses are on Lombard street and its cross streets.

The rents paid by the Negroes are without doubt far above their means and often from one-fourth to three-fourths of the total income of a family goes in rent. This leads to much non-payment of rent both intentional and unintentional, to frequent shifting of homes, and above all to stinting the families in many necessities of life in order to live in respectable dwellings. Many a Negro family eats less than it ought for the sake of living in a decent house.

Some of this waste of money in rent is sheer ignorance and carelessness. The Negroes have an inherited distrust of banks and companies, and have long neglected to take part in Building and Loan Associations. Others are simply careless in the spending of their money and lack the shrewdness and business sense of differently trained peoples. Ignorance and carelessness however will not explain all or even the greater part of the problem of rent among Negroes. There are three causes of even greater importance: these are the limited localities where Negroes may rent, the peculiar connection of dwelling and occupation among Negroes and the social organization of the Negro. The undeniable fact that most Philadelphia white people prefer not to live near Negroes limits the Negro very seriously in his choice of a home and especially in the choice of a cheap home. Moreover, real estate agents knowing the limited supply usually raise the rent a dollar or two for Negro tenants, if they do not refuse them altogether. Again, the occupations which the Negro follows, and which at present he is compelled to follow, are of a sort that makes it necessary for him to live near the best portions of the city; the mass of Negroes are in the economic world purveyors to the rich -- working in private houses, in hotels, large stores, etc. In order to keep this work they must live near by; the laundress cannot bring her Spruce street family's clothes from the Thirtieth Ward, nor can the waiter at the Continental Hotel lodge in Germantown. With the mass of white workmen this same necessity of living near work, does not hinder them from getting cheap dwellings; the factory is surrounded by cheap cottages, the foundry by long rows of houses, and even the white clerk and shop girl can, on account of their hours of labor, afford to live further out in the suburbs than the black porter who opens the store. Thus it is clear that the nature of the Negro's work compels him to crowd into the centre of the city much more than is the case with the mass of white working people. At the same time this necessity is apt in some cases to be overestimated, and a few hours of sleep or convenience serve to persuade a good many families to endure poverty in the Seventh Ward when they might be comfortable in the Twenty-fourth Ward. Nevertheless much of the Negro problem in this city finds adequate explanation when we reflect that here is a people receiving a little lower wages than usual for less desirable work, and compelled, in order to do that work, to live in a little less pleasant quarters than most people, and pay for them somewhat higher rents. . . .

## THE PHILADELPHIA RING
### 1904

Lincoln Steffens in his muckraking exposé, The
Shame of the Cities, revealed the rampant dis-
honesty of municipal politics. In his article on
Philadelphia he demonstrated that despite the
Bullitt Bill, a Republican ring was taking advantage of an apathetic electorate and exploiting the
city for its private advantage.

Source: Lincoln Steffens, The Shame of the Cities, New York: McClure
Phillips and Co., 1904.

Other American cities, no matter how bad their own condition may be, all
point with scorn to Philadelphia as worse -- "the worst-governed city in the
country." St Louis, Minneapolis, Pittsburg submit with some patience to
the jibes of any other community; the most friendly suggestion from Philadelphia is rejected with contempt. The Philadelphians are "supine,"
"asleep"; hopelessly ring-ruled, they are "complacent." "Politically be-
nighted," Philadelphia is supposed to have no light to throw upon a state of
things that is almost universal.

This is not fair. Philadelphia is, indeed, corrupt; but it is not without significance. Every city and town in the country can learn something
from the typical political experience of this great representative city. New
York is excused for many of its ills because it is the metropolis, Chicago
because of its forced development; Philadelphia is our "third largest" city
and its growth has been gradual and natural. Immigration has been blamed
for our municipal conditions; Philadelphia, with 47 per cent. of its population native-born of native-born parents, is the most American of our greater
cities. It is "good," too, and intelligent. I don't know just how to measure
the intelligence of a community, but a Pennsylvania college professor who
declared to me his belief in education for the masses as a way out of political corruption, himself justified the "rake-off" of preferred contractors
on public works on the ground of a "fair business profit." Another plea we
have made is that we are too busy to attend to public business, and we have
promised, when we come to wealth and leisure, to do better. Philadelphia
has long enjoyed great and widely distributed prosperity; it is the city of
homes; there is a dwelling house for every five persons, -- men, women,
and children, -- of the population; and the people give one a sense of more
leisure and repose than any community I ever dwelt in. Some Philadelphians
account for their political state on the ground of their ease and comfort.
There is another class of optimists whose hope is in an "aristocracy" that
is to come by and by; Philadelphia is surer that it has a "real aristocracy"

than any other place in the world, but its aristocrats, with few exceptions, are in the ring, with it, or of no political use. Then we hear that we are a young people and that when we are older and "have traditions," like some of the old countries, we also will be honest. Philadelphia is one of the oldest of our cities and treasures for us scenes and relics of some of the noblest traditions of "our fair land." Yet I was told how once, "for a joke," a party of boodlers counted out the "divvy" of their graft in unison with the ancient chime of Independence Hall.

Philadelphia is representative. This very "joke," told, as it was, with a laugh, is typical. All our municipal governments are more or less bad, and all our people are optimists. Philadelphia is simply the most corrupt and the most contented. Minneapolis has cleaned up, Pittsburg has tried to, New York fights every other election, Chicago fights all the time. Even St. Louis has begun to stir (since the elections are over), and at the worst was only shameless. Philadelphia is proud; good people there defend corruption and boast of their machine. My college professor, with his philosophic view of "rake-offs," is one Philadelphia type. Another is the man, who, driven to bay with his local pride, says: "At least you must admit that our machine is the best you have ever seen."

Disgraceful? Other cities say so. But I say that if Philadelphia is a disgrace, it is a disgrace not to itself alone, nor to Pennsylvania, but to the United States and to American character. For this great city, so highly representative in other respects, is not behind in political experience, but ahead, with New York. Philadelphia is a city that has had its reforms. Having passed through all the typical stages of corruption, Philadelphia reached the period of miscellaneous loot with a boss for chief thief, under James McManes and the Gas Ring 'way back in the late sixties and seventies. This is the Tweed stage of corruption from which St. Louis, for example, is just emerging. Philadelphia, in two inspiring popular revolts, attacked the Gas Ring, broke it, and in 1885 achieved that dream of American cities -- a good charter. The present condition of Philadelphia, therefore, is not that which precedes, but that which follows reform, and in this distinction lies its startling general significance. What has happened since the Bullitt Law or charter went into effect in Philadelphia may happen in any American city "after reform is over."

For reform with us is usually revolt, not government, and is soon over. Our people do not seek, they avoid self-rule, and "reforms" are spasmodic efforts to punish bad rulers and get somebody that will give us good government or something that will make it. A self-acting form of government is an ancient superstition. We are an inventive people, and we all think that we shall devise some day a legal machine that will turn out good government automatically. The Philadelphians have treasured this belief longer than the rest of us and have tried it more often. Throughout their history they have sought this wonderful charter and they thought they had it when they got the Bullitt Law, which concentrates in the mayor ample power, executive and political, and complete responsibility. Moreover, it calls for very little thought and action on the part of the people. All they expected to have to do when the Bullitt Law went into effect was to elect as mayor a good business man, who, with his probity and common sense, would give them that good business administration which is the ideal of many reformers.

The Bullitt Law went into effect in 1887. A committee of twelve -- four men from the Union League, four from business organizations, and four from the bosses -- picked out the first man to run under it on the Republican ticket, Edwin H. Fitler, an able, upright business man, and he was elected. Strange to say, his administration was satisfactory to the citizens, who speak well of it to this day, and to the politicians also; Boss McManes (the ring was broken , not the boss) took to the next national convention from Philadelphia a delegation solid for Fitler for President of the United States. It was a farce, but it pleased Mr. Fitler, so Matthew S. Quay, the State boss, let him have a complimentary vote on the first ballot. The politicians "fooled" Mr. Fitler, and they "fooled" also the next business mayor, Edwin S. Stuart, likewise a most estimable gentleman. Under these two administrations the foundation was laid for the present government of Philadelphia, the corruption to which Philadelphians seemed so reconciled, and the machine which is "at least the best you have ever seen."

The Philadelphia machine isn't the best. It isn't sound, and I doubt if it would stand in New York or Chicago. The enduring strength of the typical American political machine is that it is a natural growth -- a sucker, but deep-rooted in the people. The New Yorkers vote for Tammany Hall. The Philadelphians do not vote; they are disfranchised, and their disfranchisement is one anchor of the foundation of the Philadelphia organization.

This is not figure of speech. The honest citizens of Philadelphia have no more rights at the polls than the negroes down South. Nor do they fight very hard for this basic privilege. You can arouse their Republican ire by talking about the black Republican votes lost in the Southern States by white Democratic intimidation, but if you remind the average Philadelphian that he is in the same position, he will look startled, then say, "That's so, that's literally true, only I never thought of it in just that way." And it is literally true.

The machine controls the whole process of voting, and practices fraud at every stage. . . .

BACK STREET LIFE: PROSTITUTION, CRIME AND
ADDICTION
1912

The phenomenal growth of Philadelphia by the
opening of the twentieth century created a housing crisis, and many of the new migrants were
forced to find shelter in furnished rooms. These
residences severed inhabitants from the moral
moorings of their past life and often engendered
all sorts of social disorders -- crime, prostitution, drug addiction, suicide. Increasingly, social scientists became interested in systemati-
cally examining the disruptive effects of urbani-
zation on individual and group behavior.

Source: "The Furnished Room Problem in Philadelphia, " A Thesis Presented to the Faculty of the Graduate School of the University of Pennsylvania
in Partial Fulfillment of the Requirement for the Degree of Doctor of Phi-
losophy, Philadelphia: 1912.

Prostitution and Crime in the District.

No attempt to picture the rooming house would be even approximately
accurate without some reference to prostitution. It bears the stamp of modern social and industrial conditions. The hosts of unmarried men of the
great industrial city living in the rooming house represent the masculine
factor; the feminine factor consists of girls and women from the midst of
the social organism who have been impelled by circumstances to make a
quasi-voluntary choice of prostitution as a means of livelihood. Speaking
generally, we have too large a number of prostitutes in the city. Some voluntarily choose a life of shame from innate perversity. Others are victims
of force or fraud; still others, of adverse social and economic conditions.
. . .

The problem of prostitution is closely connected with that of the movement of population towards the city. A great part of the population of a modern city consists of young men who have drifted hither from the country and
small towns, attracted by the greater opportunities of rising in social life
and by the greater degree of personal comfort that the city offers. As a
rule, the income a young man earns, while sufficient to procure for himself the necessities of life and, at times, some luxuries, does not suffice
for founding a family. As his income increases, his standard of personal
comfort rises; accordingly he postpones marriage until a date in the inde-
finite future, or abandons expectation of it altogether. His interests centre
almost wholly in himself. He is responsible only to himself and the pleas-

ure he can obtain becomes the chief end of his life. It is not unnatural, then, that the strongest impulse of man should find expression in the only way open -- indulgence in vice. The rooming house district is filled with places where he may have his desires gratified. The _Evening Item_ of March 11, 1911, had forty-one ads in the "Personals" giving the locations of "massage parlors," which were nothing more nor less than houses of prostitution. "Mass. Young Operators", "Mass. Bath, Two New Attendants", "Mass. New Young Expert", "Mass. Entirely New", "Mass. Magnetic Treatment", "Mass. Satisfaction","Mass. Bath, New Nurse", "Mass. Bath, New French Nurse" -- are some of the ads. Most of the addresses given are in the district under consideration. Besides the "massage parlors" there are a number of well-known houses of ill-fame in the district. They have existed for years. Houses of assignation are very common in this district, where men and women rent a room temporarily. Such houses are found on Cherry street between Twelfth and Broad. A stranger walking from Twelfth to Broad street on Cherry after eight in the evening is likely to be accosted by a score of young girls walking the streets for purposes of prostitution. It is so patent that there is a strong suspicion that the whole system is organized, controlled and protected by powerful interests.

Prostitution appears under different guises. There are a considerable number of regular houses of prostitution. Wood street is filled with dens of the vilest character. Women call to passers-by on the street and invite them in. On a Sunday afternoon in September, 1910, the writer passed down Wood street and saw the Salvation Army hold services in the centre of the street. While the members of the Army were kneeling in the street in prayer, the inhabitants of the houses were calling out and soliciting some of the bystanders and using some of the vilest language. Darien street from Vine to Buttonwood is filled with houses of prostitution of the vilest character. Other such houses are found in the midst of the furnished room district. The best of these houses are ostensibly elegant and very quiet residences. They are almost absolutely quiet during the day, and even at night they are careful not to invite police surveillance by noise or by lighted windows. They are also very careful not to incur the ill-will of their neighbors. The existence of a notorious house of prostitution a few doors removed from a certain "Settlement House" in the district seemed to annoy the resident workers of the Settlement. They determined on its removal. But it was not as easy a matter as they had supposed. The police were very willing to do all they could, but they had to be supplied with evidence. It is pretty hard to get evidence in cases of this kind. The business men and little shop-keepers in the neighborhood did not want "this good woman disturbed." Not a parent in the neighborhood seemed desirous of having anything done in the matter. The house is still a fixed institution in the district.

Another type of disreputable house is conducted under the guise of a "rooming house" or an apartment house. It is very likely to have its street number posted in large letters on the front door, and perhaps in the window.

No one acquainted with the district denies the existence of the social evil here. It is found here rather than elsewhere because there is no neighborhood feeling here. The main-external check upon a man's conduct, the opinion of his neighbors, which has such a powerful influence in the country or small town, tends to disappear in the great city. In the rooming district there are no neighbors. No man knows the doings of even his close friends, few care what the secret life of their friends and neighbors may be. There is no community interest that can be aroused in this district. Reform is impossible, because the advocates of better conditions are not those living in the community, but fashionable residents and reformers from the suburbs. A few lament the fact that things are not as they once were, or that "people" are very wicked in our "age," but seem hopeless to remedy this state of affairs. The small shopkeepers lament the fact that their children must be reared amid such vile surroundings, yet, are careful not to molest these houses of ill-fame for fear of losing their trade. The prostitute is a liberal spender, and makes most of her purchases in her own neighborhood. The policemen know of the existence of these houses, but rarely make any arrests. Legal proof is absolutely necessary for placing a woman in such a class and branding her as a prostitute. Such proof must necessarily in the majority of cases be difficult, if not impossible, to obtain. . . .

If prostitution is denied the right of flaunting itself in public places it will take refuge in private houses. This is what has occurred in Philadelphia. From time to time there have been inns, hotels and rooming houses in the city in which no attempt has been made to conform to the rules of morality of the general community. Rooming house keepers of unscrupulous character have winked at disreputable practices when they have not positively encouraged them and shared the resulting profits. It is easy to go a step further and understand the transition from such houses that wink at loose practices to the house of assignation, which does not derive any part of its returns from the legitimate service of keeping roomers, but depends upon the patronage brought to it by the professional street walker. Wherever solicitation upon the street is permitted, such establishments will exist. Depending entirely upon vice, their location is necessarily limited to the quarters where the volume of vice is considerable. Solicitation upon the street is in turn limited to the vicinty of such houses, since the street-walker, in order to ply her vocation with profit, must have a place in the near vicinity to which she may bring her victims.

It is impossible to form any idea of the number of thefts and robberies, since the victims do not usually make complaint. It is known, however, that such crimes do take place. . . .

### Use of Cocaine.

Closely associated with the subject of prostitution is the use of drugs and cocaine. Startling revelations concerning the use of cocaine by inhabitants of this district were made in the spring of 1910. Two young men in the district made a confession, throwing an inside light on the effects of the cocaine habit. Both men had just passed their twenty-third birthday, yet asserted that they had been using morphine and cocaine for seven or eight years. Both made their confessions in matter of fact tones, telling as simply as if speaking of the weather, how young boys and girls drifted into the habit,and once slaves of the desire, would commit any crime to obtain the "dope"; how they lost all sense of decency, all regard for law and all sense of responsibility. Cocaine is taken to relieve the intense depression produced by indulgence in morphine. Cocaine is an alkeloid derived from coca leaves. The hydrochlorate which is that sold among the "dope fiends" is excellent as a local anesthetic, being made into a solution and injected at the point to be affected. It produces temporary insensibility to pain, and in the hands of an expert surgeon leaves no disagreeable after effects. The very qualities which make the drug effective as an anesthetic, however, make it harmful as an ordinary stimulant. Its prolonged use wrecks the mind and body and causes muscular twitching and insomnia. Druggists were arrested for selling it to children in this crusade. Later they were tried and convicted. The pallid faces, the drooping eyelids of numberless men and women to be seen on the streets tell a ghastly story. Cocaine fiends are usually victims of the morphine habit before they begin the use of cocaine. Prostitutes and persons whose systems are jaded use these drugs to get some of their former energy back. There is usually an unnatural life that antedates the beginning of the drug habit.

This crusade against cocaine and morphine was begun by the State Pharmaceutical Board early in 1910. In less than three months one hundred arrests were made, all of which have since been tried and convictions obtained in nearly every case. During the trials it was shown that a well organized "Cocaine Syndicate" existed in Philadelphia's Tenderloin. Children of the public schools had purchased this fatal drug and had become "sniffers" of "coke." Dr. Joseph P. Remington, dean of the College of Pharmacy, is responsible for the statement that many children of the crowded sections touching the Tenderloin and "rooming" quarters, are addicted to the cocaine habit.

I insert an extract from the Press of April 2, 1910. "The startling discovery has just been made that the drug is being used extensively by children. It is said that those who have become fiends first used cocaine put up in the form of a catarrh cure. Some years ago, before the food and drugs acts of 1906 became a law, many so-called cures for catarrh were put up in the form of a patented article. It is a known fact that cocaine has some effect upon the mucous membranes, and to those who first used the "medicine" some relief was afforded. After having used several boxes the unsuspecting victim became a slave to the habit. The so-called cure had done its work, and the victim, in search of relief from one disease, found himself in the toils of another. . . .

## PHILADELPHIA DURING THE DEPRESSION
### 1930

During the early years of the Great Depression,
when Philadelphia was blanketed in economic gloom
and the ranks of the jobless corps were swollen to
200, 000, Communist organizers stormed City Hall
in an abortive attempt to foment a Marxist revolution.

Source: The New York Times, February 15, 1930.

Philadelphia, Feb. 14 -- City Hall Plaza became a battleground soon after
noon today when about 250 members of the communistic organizations began a demonstration designed to point out, according to its leaders, that
"while the manufacturers are reaping huge profits and Mayor Mackey goes
on vacation trips there are 200, 000 unemployed workers in the city of Philadelphia."

During a fifteen-minute engagement with 150 patrolmen, detectives
and mounted policemen two of the paraders were sent to hospitals and se-
venteen were arrested.

Detective Lieutenant Jacob Gomborrow, in charge of the radical squad,
informed Superintendent Mills at 11 o'clock this morning that the demonstration, originally planned for Feb. 26, had been moved up to coincide
with the return of Mayor Mackey from a trip to the West Indies.

When the marchers left the headquarters of the Trade Union Unity
League forty-five minutes later, they were escorted by a troop of mounted
policemen who had been instructed to "lay off" until the order was given for
action.

Arrived at City Hall, the paraders, including both men and women, who
carried placards reading, "Organize and Fight, " "We Want Work" and
"Down With Politicians, " formed a wide circle and sang the "Internationale."
The next part of the plan, it was said, was to have a group ascend the stairs
to interview Mayor Mackey, who had watched the demonstration from a
window of his office.

As the crowd shouted, "To the Mayor, to the Mayor!" and as some of
its members rushed forward, the police went into action. As clubs and
fists were swung, several persons went down, including Assistant Superintendent of Police James Hearn, but by the end of fifteen minutes all of the
demonstrators who were not loaded into three patrol wagons had scattered.

Left behind were a battalion of disheveled policemen and a quantity of
literature which had been intended for distribution. It called attention to a
plan of the Communist party to stage unemployment demonstrations in every
city in the country on Feb. 26, and added: "Have all the unemployed join

councils of the Trade Union Unity League and join the demonstration at factory gates and civic centers."

Those who were taken to the hospitals for treatment later joined their companions in City Hall police cells to await a hearing tomorrow morning.
. . .

Superintendent Mills said tonight that Philadelphia police ordinarily tried to ignore "these Reds," but that "when they deliberately began to attack officers and incite to riot it is a different matter."

E. Gardos, district organizer for the Communist party in this district, said the demonstration was organized by the Council of Unemployed of the Trade Union Unity League.

## URBAN RENEWAL
### 1957

At the close of World War II, the Pennsylvania legislature attempted to reconstruct the slums of Philadelphia by passing the Pennsylvania Urban Redevelopment Law. The city, in turn, undertook many projects to eradicate the blight of the metropolis. In January 1954 a program was launched to rehabilitate the decaying neighborhood of Germantown. Beginning with a pocket project of two blocks, settlement workers involved the residents in a community effort to redress the problems of their area. Using a cooperative approach of residents and city agencies, a significant experiment was made in urban renewal. The following is a progress report published in 1957.

Source: A Neighborhood Acts: An Experiment in Cooperative Neighborhood Rehabilitation. Sponsored by Morton Neighborhood Council in Cooperation with the Office of Philadelphia's Development Coordinator and Assisted by the Staff of the Germantown Settlement, New York: Published by the National Federation of Settlements and Neighborhood Centers, Inc., May, 1957.)

It was the creation of a small playground on a formerly trash-littered vacant lot that dramatized the good which could be accomplished through cooperative effort. Led on by the enthusiasm of a few mothers and grandmothers, who clearly saw the need and were willing to roll up their sleeves, several fathers and teen-agers joined in to make the project a success. It required two years of hard work and the overcoming of numerous obstacles and disappointments to put the Tot-Lot in operation. This included raising more than $1500, leveling and clearing the land, erecting a stone wall and fence, installing equipment, and hiring a summertime supervisor. Strangely enough, this project, which has captured the imagination of the neighborhood and shown what can be done through cooperative effort, is still in dire need of more leadership and wider support. It frequently happens that community betterment programs lose some of their appeal when families are faced with more immediate social and economic problems.

Securing one-way streets and needed traffic lights were other visible signs of the neighborhood's efforts to cope with one of its most serious problems. These represented just the beginning of hard-won, block-by-block attempts to eradicate environmental nuisances created by years of neighborhood neglect and indifference. Laxity on the part of law-enforcement agencies had also contributed its share to the downward spiral. But these evidences of physical blight were precisely the kinds of problems which brought neighbors out to Council and block meetings to voice complaints and to consider constructive action. One block alone listed twenty-five grievances.

Much had to be learned about techniques in working for solutions. Again the cooperative approach was always considered first, and usually it worked. Non-controversial problems were the easiest for getting responsible participation, although in many instances several months were required to achieve the desired results. Neighbors were much more timid and frequently afraid to attack nuisances and law violations where friends and people of power and prestige were involved. Visits to City Hall, meetings with officials, and attending zoning hearings proved much easier than opposing the way a neighbor operates his business or parks his trucks on the street.

There is a third type of problem which, over a period of years, has gained conditional acceptance. This is the kind of problem created by the junk yards, slaughter houses and other non-conforming land uses which have been granted zoning variances. Elimination of these will require City action, which is already contemplated.

In the many instances where the block organizations have run into a stone wall, the Planning Committee, and sometimes the Council, have provided a new course for successful action. Further failure results in a request for help from the Development Coordinator. For example, three block groups have given up hope of getting help on problems directly caused by the Reading Railroad's passing through the area. At this point, the Coordinator's office is using its influence to arrange a meeting with a top official. In another situation, endless hours of neighbors' time and police efforts have failed to curb the flourishing illegal liquor activity. One person, mainly responsible, is known to all the community, and his record shows more than thirty arrests. There have been two convictions with light fines which have been brought about only this past year. Recently he has been apprehended twice again and awaits further trial. Minimum fines and admonishments from the magistrate will never convince this man to pull up stakes. He symbolizes successful law violation in the area. Naturally he finds it profitable to continue. Largely because of fear, neighborhood reaction has come slowly. Now, thoroughly aroused and with greater courage, the neighbors are seeking top-level support from the Police Commissioner and the District Attorney's office. Again the Development Coordinator's office has become involved.

Progress in solving such environmental problems is evident everywhere.

1. The Tot Lot is operating under supervision.

2. A substandard recreation center has been closed, and integration of its clientele in a nearby Class A facility has taken place. There has been some carry-over of interest by Negro parents to the newly organized advisory committee.

3. The vacated, rundown, recreation building has been purchased and rehabilitated by the owner of a thriving light industry. It is still available for neighborhood meetings, and its changed appearance has made a great improvement. Hopefully it may become a source of neighborhood employment. . . .

ROOTS of the RACE RIOT
1964

In 1964 Quaker City's long history of discrimination against
black people exploded into one of the worst race riots to rock
the United States. Many concerned citizens sought explanations
for the eruption. The first selection, written for the Community
Renewal Program, examines the continuing pattern of housing
segregation that has been the bane of Philadelphia's black community; the second, prepared for the United States Commission
on Civil Rights, explores the way in which police brutality has
undermined the confidence of blacks and Puerto Ricans in the
city's system of justice.

Source: Charles Abrams, The Negro Housing Problem: A Program for
Philadelphia, Philadelphia: Published by the City of Philadelphia in
Connection with the Federal Requirement on Equal Opportunity in
Housing, December, 1966; and A Report to the United States Commission
on Civil Rights. Police-Community Relations in Philadelphia, by the
Pennsylvania State Committee to the Commission, Philadelphia: 1972.

UNEQUAL HOUSING

Housing and Employment                The Negro's housing problem
                                      and his economic handicaps are
                                      closely interwoven. Lack of hous-
                                      ing, overcrowding and excessive
rents keep the Negro from putting down roots in areas of opportunity.
They limit his freedom to move more than the white man's. With
industries heading toward the city's periphery, the Negro's journey
to work and its cost are increased so that he tends to confine himself
to in-city jobs. When an industry far from the ghetto offers a Negro
work, he often turns it down because of inability to find an accessible
home. One of the main objections asserted by the nation's airlines
to the hiring of Negro hostesses, for example, has been that they
would encounter difficulty in finding housing along the routes. Poor
housing often leads to a poor home life which in turn has made employers
feel that Negroes "lack middle class virtues and responsibilities because
their home life has a lot to do with it." Other employers refuse to
hire Negroes because they fear they might settle in the community and
arouse the wrath of white homeowners. Poorer schools in the city
ghetto and inaccess to better suburban schools because of housing
exclusion limit the educational prospects of the Negro child and impair
his equipment for life. Because of the close relationship between
housing and employment and also because poor housing, poor educational
opportunities and poor environment affect the social as well as economic

life of the Philadelphia Negro family, its housing problem has become one of the primary factors in the struggle for progress and equality. . . .

## POLICE BRUTALITY

The use of excessive and/or unwarranted force by Philadelphia police was a theme that was repeated throughout Pennsylvania State Committee's open meeting and its executive sessions.

A young black man described how he arrived home in a friend's car. He and the friend were approached by a police officer as they stopped near his home. The officer began questioning his friend and the witness decided to go into his house. The policeman ordered him to return. The witness asked why. The policeman answered because he, that policeman, said so. The witness said that he was pushed and pulled, struck several times, pushed up against his friend's car, hand-cuffed, and then threatened by the policeman who had pulled his gun.

Just prior to this the witness had asked a young boy who was nearby to go to his house and ask his mother to come to the door. At about the same time, he noticed that a woman passerby had stopped and was watching while the policeman grabbed him and pushed him around.

When the young man's mother saw the policeman with his pistol on her son, she hollered: "What's going on?" The officer replied: I'm arresting this fellow." His mother then said: "Well, go ahead, arrest him; that's my son, but you don't have to pull your gun on him like that." The policeman then holstered his weapon and the mother went back into the house and called the district police station. The arresting officer was a highway patrolman.

When the officers from the district arrived, the highway patrolman allegedly continued his physical abuse of the witness and had to be restrained by the district officers. The reason for the patrolman's original approach, a burglary report, seemed to have been forgotten. Once the incident was underway, the original reason for the arrest was never mentioned.

Charges against the witness were dismissed, however. It was alleged that the police attempted to get him to promise not to file charges against the arresting officer. He refused to do this.

Edwin Wolf reported the results of a survey that his organization had made of the shooting of civilians by Philadelphia policemen during 1970. According to Mr. Wolf, 35 civilians, including a policeman's wife were shot by officers. Another civilian was killed when he was hit on the head with a blackjack and a pistol butt by a policeman. Mr. Wolf emphasized a significant point in the data, i.e., the number of young blacks who were shot by police in situations in which, he said, "there was no danger of any harm to the policeman.". . .

MAYOR TATE ON URBAN RENEWAL
1964

At the Annual Conference of United States Mayors, James H.J.
Tate, Philadelphia's chief executive, addressed the meeting and
related his city's strides forward in urban renewal and downtown revival.

Source: "Workshop: Renewing Downtown," City Problems of 1964: Proceedings, 1964 Annual Conference of Mayors, ed. Wilbur H. Baldinger,
Washington, United States Conference of Mayors, 1964.

The physical and literal heart of the city is its central area. Here,
whether described as downtown, uptown, the Loop, or merely as center
city, the great forces of commerce are concentrated in banks, department
stores and shops. The forces of industry are channeled through headquarters in office buildings. The professions, education, vast cultural
resources, research and medical centers -- all the very reasons for the
existence of the city -- are to be found. What happens downtown affects
every citizen intimately. Here the city is governed -- here the entire
package is put together and made to work. Just as blood flows through
the human heart, so the life blood of the city flows through the downtown
district.

In my own City of Philadelphia, more than one million people travel
downtown daily to work, shop, learn, eat or be entertained. Increasing
numbers are coming downtown to live in townhouses and apartment.
Philadelphia is a city of two million, and it stands in the center region
of four and one-half million people, encompassing eight counties in two
states.

In order to keep this heart pumping productively, about $100 million
of federal and city direct renewal funds provided the necessary seed money
for renewal work which is now under way to the tune of $1.5 billion.

Decisions are being made every day by businessmen who are
responsible for locating millions of dollars of capital investment. Whether
these go to strengthen center city or are disbursed throughout the region
and beyond will depend on the practical fact of the richness of the physical
facilities of downtown. It will depend also on the type of symbol downtown
represents in the minds of the people who live in the region.

All of our planning has been based on the initiative potential of the
private enterprise system. Government activity is restricted to the absolute minimum necessary to provide a framework which stimulates the
imagination of private investors and which includes the facilities necessary to support those investments after they are made. . . .

There are a number of our planning principles and practices which
I believe are worth reviewing, for they have made our work in downtown
Philadelphia meaningful and productive and, above all, supportable by
the business and banking fraternity and the community at large:

(1) Planning is economic. It is designed to retain business, trade and homes and to add new residential and commercial facilities. It is geared to conserve and build the supply of jobs and investment opportunities.

(2) It is practical. It is within the framework of our six-year capital program, adopted each year by the City Council -- a schedule of what the city can afford with no increase in taxes. At the same time, through the carefully coordinated efforts of government and private enterprise, an amazing amount of the total work in downtown, as outlined in our comprehensive plan, is already accomplished or under way and does not work to the prejudice of the total renewal activity.

(3) It is functional. The planning for downtown embraces a logical expression of regional considerations, particularly the regional transportation systems. Unified rail and bus terminal facilities will be constructed, and connections with the entire metropolitan region will be possible through coordinated regional efforts.

(4) It is culturally rich, respecting and enhancing historical landmarks and embellished by gardens and works of art. Our plans are built upon the original concept of William Penn, and they attempt to carry forward into our present day the clarity and simplicity of his idea for Philadelphia.

Finally, downtown must be attractive and exciting. Center city can survive only if people want to be there -- if they can enjoy themselves, have fun and laugh, as well as earn a living and be inspired.

I say with some pride that the Philadelphia downtown story can certainly be told in terms of rates of investment, tax return, land planning and sound fiscal management. . . .

## BIBLIOGRAPHY

A complete compilation of the literature about Philadelphia is truly encyclopedic. Therefore, this bibliography is not an exhaustive survey of the books and magazine articles concerning the Quaker City but rather a highly selective list of suggestions to students who wish to examine a particular area of interest more fully. Additional titles on almost every topic touching the history of Philadelphia can be found in Norman B. Wilkinson's Bibliography of Pennsylvania History, George Morgan's bibliographical guide in The City of Firsts as well as in the listings of articles and book reviews published by the Pennsylvania Magazine of History and Biography, Pennsylvania History, the American Historical Review, Social Science and Humanities Index, the Readers' Guide to Periodical Literature, and Writings in American History.

For those interested in working with primary source material, a rich harvest can be reaped of both public and private collections in the various libraries and historical societies located in the Philadelphia metropolitan area. The Free Library of Philadelphia houses an outstanding collection of newspapers, books and pamphlets useful for the study of local history. For students concerned with the development of the city's port, industries, and government, its public schools, charitable activities, and transportation services, an invaluable number of documents can be discovered in the Municipal branch of this library. In addition, the Ridgeway branch contains a vast number of books, portraits, and rare documents about Philadelphia.

One of the most important collections of original source material, especially the writings of Benjamin Franklin, can be found in the American Philosophical Society, located on Independence Square. Also important are the Historical Society of Pennsylvania and the Geneological Society.

## A SELECTED BIBLIOGRAPHY

Abbot, George M. A Short History of the Library Company of Philadelphia.
Philadelphia: Library Company of Philadelphia, 1913. A short and
sympathetic treatment.

Adams, Donald R., Jr. "The Bank of Stephen Girard, 1812-1831." Journal of Economic History (December, 1972).

——————————. "Wage Rates in the Early National Period: Philadelphia, 1785-1830." Journal of Economic History (September, 1968).

Aldbridge, Alfred Owen. "Benjamin Franklin and the Pennsylvania Gazette."
Proceedings of the American Philosophical Society (February, 1962).

Allinson, Edward Pease and Penrose, Boies. Philadelphia 1681-1887: A
History of Municipal Development. Philadelphia: Allen, Lane and
Scott, 1887. More instructive for what it reveals of late nineteenth
century political thought than for its narrative survey of Philadelphia's
development.

American Philosophic Society, Philadelphia. Historic Philadelphia from the
Founding until the Early Nineteenth Century: Papers Dealing with Its
People and Buildings. Philadelphia: 1953. A useful survey of historic
houses and social customs in the Quaker City.

Baisnée, Jules A. and Meng, John J. "Philadelphia and the Revolution."
American Catholic Historical Society Record, LVI (1945), 307-328;
LVII (1946), 23-40, 88-96, 179-190, 237-247; LVIII (1947), 103-106,
144-153, 214-228; LIX (1948), 241-254.

Balch, Thomas W. The Philadelphia Assemblies. Philadelphia: Allen,
Land and Scott, 1916. A monograph that affords many insights into
Philadelphia's political life.

Baldwin, Fred D. "Smedley D. Butler and Prohibition Enforcement in Philadelphia, 1924-1925." Pennsylvania Magazine of History and Biography
(July, 1960).

Baltzell, Edward Digby. Philadelphia Gentlemen; The Making of a National
Upper Class. New York: Free Press, 1966. A scholarly study from
a sociological point of view.

Barton, George. Little Journeys around Old Philadelphia. Philadelphia:

Peter Reilly Co., 1925. The old landmarks of Philadelphia, vividly
presented in amusing anecdotes and quotations from original sources.

_____. Walks and Talks about Old Philadelphia. Philadelphia:
Peter Reilly Co., 1928. A diverting, gossipy book of anecdotes about Philadelphia's famous people and historic buildings.

Bell, Whitfield Jenks. "Science and Humanity in Philadelphia, 1775-1790."
Ann Arbor: University Microfilms, 1947. A solid monograph on the
Quaker City's intellectual life prepared as a doctoral dissertation at
the University of Pennsylvania.

_____. "The Scientific Environment of Philadelphia, 1775-
1790." American Philosophic Society Proceedings. XCII (1948), 6-14.

Biddle, Cordelia Drexel. My Philadelphia Father. Garden City, N.Y.:
Doubleday, 1955. A popular memoir.

Biddle, Francis. A Casual Past. Garden City, N.Y.: Doubleday, 1961.
A positive profile of the city.

Biddle, George. An American Artist's Story. New York: Little Brown
and Company, 1939. The beginning chapters are replete with material
about Philadelphia's social conditions.

Binzen, Peter. Whitetown, U.S.A. New York: Random, 1970. A reporter's investigation into the ethnically mixed neighborhood of Kensington
where hard-working homeowners are bent upon preserving an 1890s
city district.

Blumin, Stuart. "Mobility and Change in Ante-Bellum Philadelphia." Nine-
teenth-Century Cities: Essays in the New Urban History. Edited by
Stephan Thernstrom and Richard Sennett. New Haven and London:
Yale University Press, 1969. A quantitative examination that explodes
early Jacksonian myths.

Bowen, Daniel. A History of Philadelphia, with Notice of Villages in the
Vicinity . . . Containing a Correct Account of the City Improvements
up to the Year 1839, Also the State of Society in Relation to Science,
Religion and Morals; with an Historical Account of the Military Operations of the Late War, Including the Names of Over Two Thousand Pa-
triotic Officers and Citizen Soldiers. Philadelphia: 1839. A journalis-
tic and miscellaneous compilation of historical information concerning
the institutions of the municipality in 1839.

Brewington, Marion V. "Maritime Philadelphia, 1609-1837." Pennsylvania
Magazine of History and Biography. LXIII (1939), 93-117.

Bridenbaugh, Carl. Cities in the Wilderness: The First Century of Urban
    Life in America, 1625-1742. New York: Ronald Press, 1938. A
    scholarly comparative study of the creation of Philadelphia and four
    other colonial cities.

——————————— Rebels and Gentlemen; Philadelphia in the Age of Frank-
    lin. New York: Oxford University Press, 1962. A first-rate, lively
    analysis of the development of American culture in Philadelphia.

Brig, Jean H. "Publishing - A Philadelphia Tradition." Pennsylvania Maga-
    zine, XXXVII, no. 5 (1950), 22-24, 42-43.

Brookhauser, Frank. Our Philadelphia; A Candid and Colorful Portrait of
    a Great City. Garden City, N.Y.: Doubleday, 1957. A haphazard,
    anecdotal profile of Philadelphia from its days of colonial leadership
    to its twentieth century status as the nation's second largest port, writ-
    ten with little critical insight.

Brown, William H. and Gilbert, Charles E. Planning Municipal Investment;
    A Case Study of Philadelphia. Philadelphia: University of Pennsylvania
    Press, 1961. An instructive analysis of municipal budgets and public
    works.

Burt, Maxwell Struthers. Philadelphia, Holy Experiment. Garden City,
    N.Y.: Doubleday, Doran and Co., 1945. A popular account in one
    volume presenting a colorful biographical survey of the city by one of
    its critical admirers.

Burt, Nathaniel. The Perennial Philadelphians; The Anatomy of an Ameri-
    can Aristocracy. Boston: Little, Brown and Co., 1963. An anecdotal
    portrait of Old Philadelphia's upper class that captures the personality
    of the city.

Burwell, Basil. "A Man for All Souls." American Heritage, (December,
    1971). A study of the Quaker minister, John Woolman, 1720-1771.

Butterfield, Roger. "Benjamin Franklin's Philadelphia." Holiday, IX
    (June, 1951), 34-35.

Calderhead, William L. "Philadelphia in Crisis, June - July, 1863." Penn-
    sylvania History (April, 1961)

Campbell, Jane. "Old Phildelphia Music." Philadelphia Historical Society
    Publication, II (1926), 181-206.

Cheyney, Edward P. History of the University of Pennsylvania, 1740-1940.
    Philadelphia: University of Pennsylvania Press, 1940. The standard
    scholarly treatment of the history of the University of Pennsylvania

during two centuries, centered primarily on the men who shaped its development.

Clark, Dennis. "A Pattern of Urban Growth: Residential Development and Church Location in Philadelphia." Records of the American Catholic Historical Society of Philadelphia (September, 1971).

——————————. "Militants of the 1860's: The Philadelphia Fenians." Pennsylvania Magazine of History and Biography (January, 1971).

Clark, Sydney P. Pennsylvania Hospital Since May 1, 1751. Two Hundred Years in Philadelphia. New York: Newcomen Society in North American, 1951. A good survey.

Collins, Herman Le Roy. Philadelphia, A Story of Progress. New York, Philadelphia: Lewis Historical Publishing Co., 1941. A multi-volume work that contains a vast quarry of information but is marred by its uncritical "chamber of commerce" spirit.

Corner, George A. (ed.) Autobiography of Benjamin Rush. Princeton, N.J.: Princeton University Press, 1948. A penetrating account by an outstanding Philadelphia physician of the 18th century.

Cornog, William H. School of the Republic 1893-1943; A Half-Century of the Central High School of Philadelphia. Philadelphia: Associated Alumni of Central High School, 1952. A detailed, partisan survey.

Cox, Harold E. and Meyers, John F. "The Philadelphia Traction Monopoly and the Pennsylvania Constitution of 1874: The Prostitution of an Ideal." Pennsylvania History (October, 1968).

Crouthamel, James L. "Three Philadelphians in the Bank War: A Neglected Chapter in American Lobbying." Pennsylvania History (October, 1960).

Crumlish, Joseph D. A City Finds Itself; the Philadelphia Home Rule Charter Movement. Detroit: Wayne State University Press, 1959. A good scholarly study.

Davies, Benjamin. Some Account of the City of Philadelphia, the Capital of Pennsylvania, and Seat of the Federal Congress; of its Civil and Religious Institutions, Population, Trade, and Government; Interspersed with Occasional Observations. Philadelphia: Printed by Richard Folwell for the Author, 1794. Primarily of interest to antiquarians.

Davis, Allen F. and Sutherland, John F. "Reform and Uplift among Philadelphia Negroes. The Diary of Helen Parrish, 1888." Pennsylvania Magazine of History and Biography (October, 1970).

Disbrow, Donald W. "Reform in Philadelphia under Mayor Blankenburg, 1912-1916." Pennsylvania History (October, 1960).

Douglas, Paul H. "Two Eighteenth Century Philadelphians: Benjamin Franklin and John Woolman." General Magazine and Historical Chronology, LIV (1952), 131-138.

Du Bois, William Edward Burghardt. The Philadelphia Negro: A Social Study. Philadelphia: University of Pennsylvania Press, 1899. A balanced sociological analysis by a pioneering black scholar.

Dusinberre, William. Civil War Issues in Philadelphia, 1856-1865. Philadelphia: University of Pennsylvania Press, 1965. An informative, scholarly monograph.

Eberlein, Harold Donaldson and Hubbard, Cortland Van Dyke. Portrait of a Colonial City, Philadelphia, 1670-1838. Philadelphia, New York: J. B. Lippincott, 1939. An antiquarian interpretation of Philadelphia's architecture that stresses geneological and social details. Richly illustrated.

Edmonds, Franklin Spencer. History of the Central High School of Philadelphia. Philadelphia: J.B. Lippincott, 1902. A sympathetic, informative study.

Ellsworth, Lucius F. "The Philadelphia Society for the Promotion of Agriculture and Agricultural Reform, 1785-1793." Agricultural History (July, 1968).

Etting, Gloria Braggiotti. Philadelphia, the Intimate City. New York: Viking Press, 1968. A beautifully photographed guidebook to the city.

Faris, John Thompson. Old Churches and Meeting Houses In and Around Philadelphia. Philadelphia and London: J.B. Lippincott, 1926. A local history which focuses on the Protestant churches of colonial Philadelphia.

——————————, The Romance of Philadelphia. Philadelphia and London: J.B. Lippincott, 1918. A prosaic treatment of the social customs of colonial and revolutionary Philadelphia.

Federal Writers' Project. Pennsylvania. Philadelphia, a Guide to the Nation's Birthplace. Philadelphia: William Penn Association, 1937. An encyclopedic reference work that describes Philadelphia's historical and cultural life with little critical discrimination.

Fox, Bonnie R. "Unemployment Relief in Philadelphia, 1930-1932: A Study
of the Depression's Impact on Voluntarism." Pennsylvania Magazine
of History and Biography (January, 1969).

Geffen, Elizabeth M. "William Henry Furness, Philadelphia Antislavery
Preacher." Pennsylvania Magazine of History and Biography (July, 1958).

Geib, George W. "The Restoration of the Port of Philadelphia, 1783-1789."
American Neptune (October, 1972).

Gerson, Robert A. Music in Philadelphia. Presser, 1940. A comprehensive musical history of the city.

Gilbert, Charles E. Governing the Suburbs. Bloomington: Indiana University Press, 1967. A serious analysis of the politics in Bucks, Mont-
gomery, and Delaware counties which adjoin Philadelphia by a political
scientist who argues that county governments provide more effective
rule than regionalism.

Gilbert, Daniel R. "Patterns of Organization and Membership in Colonial
Philadelphia Club Life, 1725-1775." University of Pennsylvania, 1952.
A doctoral dissertation.

Gillingham, Harrold E. "Calico and Linen Printing in Philadelphia." Pennsylvania Magazine of History and Biography, LII (1928), 97-110.

———————————. "Some Colonial Ships Built in Philadelphia." Pennsylvania Magazine of History and Biography, LVI (1932), 156-186.

———————————. "Philadelphia's First Fire Defense." Pennsylvania
Magazine of History and Biography, LVI (1932), 355-377.

———————————. "Some Early Philadelphia Instrument Makers."
Pennsylvania Magazine of History and Biography, LI (1927), 289-308.

Govan, Thomas Payne. Nicholas Biddle. Chicago: University of Chicago
Press, 1959. A revisionist account of the famous Philadelphia banker
by a scholar who emphasizes the accomplishments of his hero.

Gray, Austin K. Benjamin Franklin's Library. A Short Account of the Library Company of Philadelphia, 1731-1931. New York: Macmillan,
1937. A succinct history of the Library Company from its colonial
days through the twentieth century, presented affectionately by a librarian of the institution.

Gray, Ralph D. "Philadelphia and the Chesapeake and Delaware Canal,

1769-1823." Pennsylvania Magazine of History and Biography, (October, 1960).

Gray, William. "Philadelphia's Architecture." Philadelphia City Historical Society Publications, no. 12 (1915), 319-376.

Greenberg, Irwin F. "Philadelphia Democrats Get a New Deal." Pennsylvania Magazine of History and Biography (April, 1973).

Hallgren, Mauritz A. "Mass Misery in Philadelphia." Nation, CXXXIV (1932), 275-277.

Henry, Frederick P. (ed.) Founders' Week Memorial Volume; Containing an Account of the Two Hundred and Twenty-fifth Anniversary of the Founding of the City of Philadelphia, and Histories of Its Principal Scientific Institutions, Medical College, Hospitals, etc. Philadelphia: 1909. Published by the city of Philadelphia in commemoration of the 225th anniversary of its founding.

_____. Standard History of the Medical Profession of Philadelphia. Chicago: Godspeed, 1897. A lengthy, competent work which provides a wealth of information on the social aspects of medicine.

Heyl, Francis. "The Battle of Germantown." Philadelphia City Historical Society Publications, no. 3 (1908), 43-64.

Hindle, Brooke. "The March of the Paxton Boys." William and Mary Quarterly, III (1946), 461-486.

_____. The Pursuit of Science in Revolutionary America, 1735-1789. Chapel Hill, N.C.: University of North Carolina Press, 1956. A brilliant analysis that includes much useful information on pioneering scientific developments in Philadelphia.

History of the Founding of Philadelphia, Some Brief Historic Chapters on the City. Philadelphia: Times Printing House, 1910.

Hunter, Robert. "The Origin of the Philadelphia General Hospital." Pennsylvania Magazine of History and Biography, LVII (1933), 32-57.

Hutson, James H. "An Investigation of the Inarticulate: Philadelphia's White Oaks." William and Mary Quarterly (January, 1971).

Issel, William H. "Modernization in Philadelphia School Reform, 1882-1905." Pennsylvania Magazine of History and Biography (June, 1970).

Jackson, Joseph. "Athens of America." American Catholic Historical Society Records, LVI (1945), 99-113.

——————————. "Birthplace of a Nation." American Catholic Historical Society Records, LIV (1943), 1-27.

——————————. Encyclopedia of Philadelphia. Harrisburg: The National Historical Association, 1931-33. A four volume encyclopedic summary of Philadelphia's noteworthy citizens, institutions, and incidents.

——————————. A History of Germantown Academy. Philadelphia: S.H. Burbank, 1910. A clear and sympathetic treatment.

James, Reese Davis. Cradle of Culture, 1800-1810; the Philadelphia Stage. Philadelphia: University of Pennsylvania Press, 1957. An admirable, scholarly monograph.

——————————. Old Drury; A History of the Philadelphia Stage, 1800-1835. Philadelphia: University of Pennsylvania Press, 1932. Primarily a scholarly reference book that makes an important contribution to the intellectual and social history of Philadelphia.

James, Sydney V. "Quaker 'Charity' before the American Revolution." Bulletin of the Friends' Historical Association (Autumn, 1961).

Jayne, Horace F. and Woodhouse, Samuel W. Jr. "Early Philadelphia Silversmiths." Art in America, IX (1921), 248-259.

Jensen, Arthur L. The Maritime Commerce of Colonial Philadelphia. Madison: State Historical Society of Wisconsin for the Department of History, University of Wisconsin, 1963. A scholarly, if not thoroughly convincing treatment of pre-revolutionary Philadelphia based primarily on mercantile correspondence and customs records.

Johnson, Gerald White. Pattern for Liberty; The Story of Old Philadelphia. New York: McGraw-Hill, 1952. A readable, illustrated portrayal of the city from Yorktown to 1800 when Philadelphia was the capital of the nation.

Johnson, Victor L. "Fair Traders and Smugglers in Philadelphia, 1754-1763." Pennsylvania Magazine of History and Biography (April, 1959).

Joyce, John St. George. Story of Philadelphia. Philadelphia: Rex,1919. An informative and conventional survey that is marred by its uncritical "booster" spirit.

King, Moses. Philadelphia and Notable Philadelphians. New York: M. King, 1902. Profusely illustrated.

Kingscella, Hazel G. "Music in Colonial Philadelphia, 1664-1776." Washington University, 1941. A doctoral dissertation.

Klein, Randolph Shipley. "Moses Bartram." Quaker History (Spring, 1968).

Korbe, Sidney. The Development of the Colonial Newspaper. Pittsburgh: Colonial Press, 1944. An extensive treatment of journalism in Philadelphia is included in this general history.

Kupferberg, Herbert. Those Fabulous Philadelphians; The Life and Times of a Great Orchestra. New York: C. Scribner's Sons, 1969. Narrated by the record critic of the Atlantic Monthly, the book eulogistically examines the history of the Philadelphia Orchestra, paying particular attention to the careers of Leopold Stokowski and Eugene Ormandy.

Lafore, Laurence Davis. Philadelphia; The Unexpected City. Garden City, N.Y.: Doubleday, 1965. A vivid and affectionate account of Philadelphia's pluralistic society, enhanced by photographs of the landmarks and daily life of the city.

La Gorce, John O. "The Historic City of Brotherly Love: Philadelphia. Born of Penn and Strengthened by Franklin, A Metropolis of Industries, Homes and Parks." National Geographic Magazine, LXII (1932), 643-697.

Lannie, Vincent P. and Diethorn, Bernard C. "For the Honor and Glory of God: The Philadelphia Bible Riots of 1840." Historical Education Quarterly (Spring, 1968).

Lawrence, Charles. Philadelphia Almshouses and Hospitals: 1701-1900. Philadelphia: C. Lawrence, 1905. A useful introductory treatment.

Leffmann, Henry. The Consolidation of Philadelphia. Philadelphia: City Historical Society of Philadelphia, 1908. A dispassionate and lucid account.

Lewis, John Frederick. The History of an Old Philadelphia Land Title. Philadelphia: Patterson and White Co., 1934.

_____. History of the Apprentices' Library of Philadelphia 1820-1920, the Oldest Circulating Library in America. Philadelphia: 1924. A sympathetic narrative, originally read at a special meeting of the Historical Society of Pennsylvania.

Lippincott, Horace Mather. Early Philadelphia; Its People, Life and Progress. Philadelphia and London: J.B. Lippincott, 1917. A lucid but uncritical tribute to the city's leading men and institutions from its founding through the middle of the eighteenth century.

Livingood, James Weston. The Philadelphia-Baltimore Trade Rivalry, 1780-1860. Harrisburg: Pennsylvania Historical and Museum Commission, 1947. An admirable analysis of urban imperialism.

Lokken, Roy N. "The Social Thought of James Logan." William and Mary Quarterly (January, 1970). An important contribution by a distinguished intellectual historian.

Macfarlane, John J. Manufacturing in Philadelphia, 1683-1912. Philadelphia: Commercial Museum, 1912. A succinct, authoritative survey of the development of industry in Philadelphia.

Mackey, Philip English. "Law and Order, 1877: Philadelphia's Response to the Railroad Riots." Pennsylvania Magazine of History and Biography (April, 1972).

Mansfield, Mary A. F. "Yellow Fever Epidemics of Philadelphia, 1699-1805." University of Pittsburgh, 1949. A master's thesis.

Matthews, Albert Franklin. What Philadelphia Is; Sketch of the Industries and Leading Characters of the City. With Special Reference to Its Historic Past. Philadelphia: J.B. Lippincott Co., 1890. A useful, though dated, local history.

Mease, James. Picture of Philadelphia, Giving an Account of Its Origin, Increase and Improvement in Arts, Sciences, Manufactures, Commerce and Revenue. With a . . . View of Its Societies . . . and Public Buildings. Philadelphia: R.Desilver, 1831. A two volume book that provides invaluable source material on the city.

Meyer, Gladys Eleanor. Free Trade in Ideas; Aspects of American Liberalism Illustrated in Franklin's Philadelphia Career. New York: King's Crown Press, 1941. A suggestive study, originally prepared as a doctoral dissertation at Columbia University.

Mishoff, Willard O. "Business in Philadelphia During the British Occupation." Pennsylvania Magazine of History and Biography, LXI (1937), 165-181.

Morgan, George. The City of Firsts, Being a Complete History of the City of Philadelphia from Its Founding in 1682, to the Present Time. Philadelphia: The Historical Publication Society, 1926. A partisan treatment that contains much valuable information.

Murphy, Lawrence W. "John Dunlap's Packet and Its Competitors." Journalism Quarterly, XXVIII (1951) 58-62.

Newburg, Judson E. "British Occupation of Philadelphia During the Winter, 1777-1778." Temple University, 1950. A master's thesis.

Nitzsche, George Erasmus. University of Pennsylvania: Its History, Traditions, Buildings and Memorials; Also a Brief Guide to Philadelphia. Philadelphia: International Printing Co., 1916. An uncritical booster tract.

Nygren, Edward J. "The First Art Schools at the Pennsylvania Academy of Fine Arts." Pennsylvania Magazine of History and Biography, (April, 1971)

Oaks, Robert F. "Big Wheels in Phiadelphia: Du Simitiere's List of Carriage Owners." Pennsylvania Magazine of History and Biography, (July, 1971)

Oberholtzer, Ellis P. "Franklin's Philosophical Society." Popular Science Monthly, LX (1902), 430-437.

————————. Philadelphia; A History of the City and Its People, A Record of 225 Years. Philadelphia, Chicago: S.J. Clarke, 1912. A scholarly, serious analysis of Philadelphia's development and of her leading citizens.

"The Origin of Street Cleaning and Street Lighting in Philadelphia." American City, XXXII (1925), 182.

Packard, Francis R. "Benjamin Franklin and the Pennsylvania Hospital." General Magazine and Historical Chronology, LXII (1940), 190-191.

————————. "The Practice of Medicine in the 18th Century. Annals of Medical History, V, (1933), 135-150.

Palmer, Gladys Louise. Philadelphia Workers in a Changing Economy. Philadelphia: University of Pennsylvania Press, 1956. A thoughtful analysis, prepared at the Industrial Research Department of the Wharton School of Finance and Commerce.

Parker, Peter. "The Philadelphia Printer: A Study of an Eighteenth Century Businessman." Business History Review (Spring, 1966).

Parsons, Wilfred. "Early Catholic Publishers in Philadelphia." Catholic
    Historical Review XXIV (1938), 141-152.

Pennell, Elizabeth Robins. Our Philadelphia. Philadelphia and London:
    J.B. Lippincott, 1914. A detailed memoir of random recollections
    based on the author's girlhood in nineteenth century Philadelphia.

Pennell, Joseph. Quaint Corners in Philadelphia, with One Hundred and
    Seventy-four Illustrations. Philadelphia, New York: J. Wanamaker,
    1899. Good for fanciers of nostalgia.

Penniman, James Hosmer. Philadelphia in the Early Eighteen Hundreds.
    Philadelphia: St. Stephen's Church, 1923. A brief introduction to the
    subject.

Pepper, George Wharton. Philadelphia Lawyer, An Autobiography. Phila-
    delphia and New York: J.B. Lippincott Co., 1944. An autobiography
    of the lawyer and senator, spanning the period 1867 to the 1940s that
    is enlivened by droll anecdotes and nostalgia for another century.

Pernick, Martin S. "Politics, Parties, and Pestilence: Epidemic Yellow
    Fever in Philadelphia and the Rise of the First Party System." William
    and Mary Quarterly (October, 1972).

Philadelphia; Its Location, Commerce, Industries, History and Points of
    Interest. Philadelphia: Philadelphia Chamber of Commerce, 1917.
    A typical booster manual.

Plummer, Wilbur C. "Consumer Credit in Colonial Philadelphia." Penn-
    sylvania Magazine of History and Biography, LXVI (1942), 385-409.

Pollock, Thomas C. The Philadelphia Theatre in the Eighteenth Century.
    Philadelphia: University of Pennsylvania Press, 1933. A detailed and
    conventional treatment.

Powell, J.H. Bring Out Your Dead. Philadelphia: University of Pennsyl-
    vania Press, 1944. An account of the cholera epidemic of 1793 and the
    role played by Benjamin Rush.

Price, Eli Kirk. The History of the Consolidation of the City of Philadelphia.
    Philadelphia: J.B. Lippincott and Co., 1873. An old but useful survey.

Pyle, Howard. "Bartram and His Garden." Harper's, LX (1880), 321-330.

Reichley, James. The Art of Government; Reform and Organization Politics
    in Philadelphia. New York: Fund for the Republic, 1959. A suggestive
    interpretation of Philadelphia politics.

Reisman, David. "The Oldest Medical School in America." General Magazine and Historical Chronology, XXXVIII (1936), 273-290.

Repplier, Agnes. Philadelphia: The Place and the People. New York: Macmillan, 1898. A reliable account by a lively essayist which lacks detailed historical analysis.

Resnik, Henry S. Turning on the System; War in the Philadelphia Public Schools. New York: Pantheon Books, 1970. Written by a free-lance reporter who pulls together the diverse elements of the Philadelphia school system and argues strongly for avant-garde educational reform.

Richardson, Edgar P. "Centennial City." American Heritage. (December, 1971). A well-written account of Philadelphia in 1876 with emphasis on the water colors of David J. Kennedy.

Richter, Thomas D. Philadelphia, Its Contributions, Its Present, Its Future. Philadelphia: Philadelphia Chamber of Commerce, 1929. A prosaic treatment that holds few surprises.

Rightmyer, Nelson W. "Churches under Enemy Occupation, Philadelphia, 1777-8." Church History, XIV (1945), 33-60.

Rivinus, Marion W.M. The Story of Rittenhouse Square, 1682-1951. Philadelphia: S.A. Wilson Co., 1951. A conventional local history with appeal to lovers of nostalgia.

Roberts, George and Mary. Triumph of Fairmount. Philadelphia: J.B. Lippincott, 1960. An account of modern Philadelphia and the role played by Fiske Kimball, told with affectionate prejudice.

Rubin, Julius. "Canal or Railroad: Imitation and Innovation in the Response to the Erie Canal in Philadelphia, Baltimore and Boston." Transactions of the American Philosophical Society, LI, Part 7 (1961)., 5-14. An important analysis of Philadelphia's conservative leadership in the crucial race for economic control of the West.

Ryon, Roderick N. "Moral Reform and Democratic Politics: The Dilemma of Robert Vaux." Quaker History (Spring, 1970). A suggestive article on the Democratic patrician mayor who played an important role in Philadelphia's history in the mid-nineteenth century.

Salter, John Thomas. Boss Rule; Portraits in City Politics. New York, London: Whittlesey House, McGraw-Hill, 1935. A provocative study of Philadelphia ward heelers by a political science professor who stresses vignettes over statistics.

Scharf, John and Westcott, Thomas. History of Philadelphia. 1609-1884. Philadelphia: L.H. Everts and Co., 1884. A thorough and fairly reliable historical treatment.

Shryock, Richard H. "A Century of Meidcal Progress in Philadelphia, 1750-1850." Pennsylvania History, VIII (1941), 7-28.

_____. Medicine and Society in America: 1660-1860 (Ithaca, N.Y.: Great Seal Books, 1960), Ch. III.

Silcox, Harry C. "Philadelphia Negro Educator: Jacob C. White, Jr., 1837-1902." Pennsylvania Magazine of History and Biography (January, 1973)

Simpson, Henry. The Lives of Eminent Philadelphians, Now Deceased. Collected from Original and Authentic Sources. Philadelphia: W. Brotherhead, 1859. Primarily of geneological interest.

Smyth, Albert Henry. The Philadelphia Magazines and Their Contributors, 1741-1850. Freeport, N.Y.: Books for Libraries Press, 1970.

Sprogle, Howard O. Philadelphia Police, Past and Present. Philadelphia: 1887. A long but fascinating study of an essential urban service from the eighteenth century to 1885.

Tatum, George Bishop. Penn's Great Town; 250 Years of Philadelphia Architecture Illustrated in Prints and Drawings. Philadelphia: University of Pennsylvania Press, 1961. A beautifully illustrated book on the history of Philadelphia's architecture.

Taylor, Frank Hamilton. Philadelphia in the Civil War 1861-1865. Illustrated from Contemporary Prints and Photographs and Drawing from the Author. Philadelphia: 1913. A valuable collection of memorabilia.

Teeters, Negley K. "The Early Days of the Philadelphia House of Refuge." Pennsylvania History (April, 1960).

Tolles, Frederick Barnes. Meeting House and Counting House; The Quaker Merchants of Colonial Philadelphia, 1682-1763. Chapel Hill, N.C.: Institute of Early American History and Culture at Williamsburg, Virginia, by the University of North Carolina Press, 1948. A stimulating examination of the conflict between worldly enterprise and the Quaker conscience in colonial Philadelphia.

Tooker, Elva. Nathan Trotter, Philadelphia Merchant, 1787-1853. Cambridge: Harvard University Press, 1955. A biography of a successful

Philadelphia merchant who changed his business from importing English merchandise to specializing in metals and commercial paper.

Turner, William L. "The College Academy and Charitable School of Philadelphia - 1740 -1779." University of Pennsylvania, 1952. A doctoral dissertation.

Van Doren, Carl. Benjamin Franklin. New York: Viking, 1958. A classic biography of Philadelphia's most eminent citizen.

Veira, M. Laffitte. West Philadelphia Illustrated, Early History of West Philadelphia and Its Environs; Its People and Its Historical Points. Philadelphia: Civil Print Co., 1903. A local history that stresses biography.

Vickers, George E. Philadelphia, the Story of an American City. Philadelphia: Dunlap Printing Co., 1893. A tribute to the city by one of its admirers.

Wainwright, Nicholas B. History of the Philadelphia National Bank; A Century and a Half of Philadelphia Banking, 1803-1953. Philadelphia: 1953. A useful introduction.

——————————— Philadelphia in the Romantic Age of Lithography; An Illustrated History of Early Lithography in Philadelphia, with a Descriptive List of Philadelphia Scenes Made by Philadelphia Lithographers Before 1866. Philadelphia: Historical Society of Pennsylvania, 1958. A vivid recreation of historic Philadelphia, stunningly illustrated.

——————————— A Philadelphia Story: 1752-1952: The Contributionship. A partisan account of the development of insurance in Philadelphia over the course of two centuries.

Wallace, John William. An Old Philadelphian, Colonel William Bradford, the Patriot Printer of 1776. Sketches of His Life. Philadelphia: Sherman and Co., 1884. A sympathetic treatment of a notable Philadelphian.

——————————— ."Early Printing in Philadelphia." Pennsylvania Magazine of History and Biography, IV (1880), 432-445.

Wallace, Philip B. Colonial Ironwork in Old Philadelphia; The Craftsmanship of the Early Days of the Republic. New York: Architectural Book Publishing Co., 1930. A profusely illustrated book that contains a mine of information on a highly specialized subject.

Walther, Rudolph J. Happenings in Ye Olde Philadelphia: 1680-1900. Philadelphia: The Author, 1925. Emphasis is placed on local color rather than critical evaluation.

Warner, Sam Bass. The Private City; Philadelphia in Three Periods of Its Growth. Philadelphia: University of Pennsylvania Press, 1968. A suggestive, carefully researched book that argues that the quest for quick profits in Philadelphia often stymied the city's response to communal needs.

Watson, John Fanning. Annals of Philadelphia and Pennsylvania, in the Olden Time; Being a Collection of Memoirs, Anecdotes, and Incidents of the City and Its Inhabitants and of the Earliest Settlements of the Inland Part of Pennsylvania. Philadelphia: E.S. Stuart, 1887. A history of the city and state that emphasizes social life and customs.

Weigley, Emma Seifrit. "The Philadelphia Chef: Mastering the Art of Philadelphia Cookery." Pennsylvania Magazine of History and Biography (April, 1972). An account of the culinary contribution of Sarah Tyson Heston Rorer, 1849-1937.

Welch, Earl. Cradle of Our Nation: Philadelphia, 1682-1949. New York: Henry Holt, 1949. Written for grades five to eight, the book presents an uninspired history of the city.

Westcott, Thompson. The Historic Mansions and Buildings of Philadelphia, with Some Notice of Their Owners and Occupants. Philadelphia: Porter and Coates, 1877. A gossipy tour through old Philadelphia.

Weygandt, Cornelius. "Old Philadelphia: Theme and Variations." General Magazine and Historical Chronology, XLI (1939), 345-354.

——————————. Philadelphia Folks; Ways and Institutions In and About the Quaker City. New York, London: D. Appleton-Century Co., 1938. A rambling and nostalgic book which lovingly describes the manners and mores of an earlier generation.

White, Charles Fred. Who's Who in Philadelphia; A Collection of Thirty Biographical Sketches of Philadelphia Colored People . . . Together with Cuts and Information of Some of Their Leading Institutions and Organizations. Philadelphia: A.M.E. Book Concern, 1912. A fascinating collection of source material.

White, Theophilus Ballou. The Philadelphia Art Alliance; Fifty Years: 1915-1965. Philadelphia: University of Pennsylvania Press, 1965. A good study.

Whiteman, Maxwell. "Isaac Leeser and the Jews of Philadelphia." Publication of the American Jewish Historical Society (June, 1959).

Williams, Churchill. "Philadelphia in Fiction." Bookman, XVI (1902), 360-373

Wilson, Janet. "The Bank of North America and Pennsylvania Politics, 1781-1787." Pennsylvania Magazine of History and Biography, LXVI (1942), 3-28.

Winslow, Stephen Noyes. Biographies of Successful Philadelphia Merchants. Philadelphia: J.K. Simon, 1864. A dated and uncritical treatment.

Wolf, Edwin. "The 1706 Charter of the City of Philadelphia." Proceedings of the American Philosophic Society, XCVI (1952), 388-405.

Woolsey, Sarah C. A Short History of the City of Philadelphia from Its Foundation to the Present Time. Boston: Roberts, 1887. A brief account that contains much useful information but lacks critical judgment.

Young, John Russell (ed.) Memorial History of the City of Philadelphia, from Its First Settlement to the Year 1895. New York: History Co., 1895-98. Howard M. Jenkins supplies an accurate, conventional history in the first volume, and George O. Seilhamer presents biographical sketches of important Philadelphians in the second volume.

Zimmerman, John J. "Benjamin Franklin and the Quaker Party, 1755-1756." William and Mary Quarterly (July, 1960).

_____. "The Sam Adams of Philadelphia." Mississippi Valley Historical Review (December, 1958).